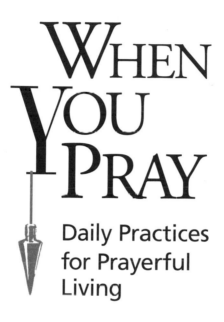

WHEN YOU PRAY

Daily Practices for Prayerful Living

Rueben P. Job

WHEN YOU PRAY
DAILY PRACTICES FOR PRAYERFUL LIVING

Copyright © 2009 by Abingdon Press

This book is printed on acid-free paper.

Library of Congress Cataloging-in-Publication Data

Job, Rueben P.
   When you pray : daily practices for prayerful living / Rueben P. Job.
      p. cm.
   ISBN 978-1-4267-0266-2 (binding: leather / fine binding/leather - imitation : alk. paper)
   1. United Methodist Church (U.S.)--Prayers and devotions. 2. Church year meditations. 3. Common lec-tionary (1992) I. Title.
   BV245.J59 2009
   242'.2--dc22

                              2009019708

10 11 12 13 14 15 16 17 18--10 9 8 7 6 5 4 3
MANUFACTURED IN CHINA

USER'S GUIDE

Welcome to your personal copy of *When You Pray: Daily Practices for Prayerful Living*. It is designed for all who seek to live faithfully and fully as followers of Jesus Christ and each part is intended to aid you in your own walk with God. Nothing in the following pages provides a magic formula to nurture your own soul, but all in the following pages is designed to place in your hands ancient and contemporary resources, that when utilized, lead to a closer and life-giving companionship with the One who loves you without limit and desires to dwell within you as a loving and wise guide, companion, and source of strength.

This resource seeks to respond to the needs we all have for a pattern of prayer that is accessible, usable, and adaptable to our diverse life experiences in our contemporary world. What you have in your hands has grown out of my discoveries as I continue to learn how to pray following the pattern of prayer that Jesus has given in the prayer he taught the disciples and in his own prayers recorded in the Gospels.

It is amazing that the disciples did not ask Jesus to teach them how to tell a parable, multiply the loaves, or heal the sick; but they did ask him to teach them how to pray. And when asked, Jesus taught them this simple and complete prayer. And the Lord's Prayer has been our pattern of prayer ever since. The disciples' request and the response of Jesus is more than a subtle reminder of the importance of prayer for them and for us. This brief prayer contains the essential elements of a healthy life of prayer and a healthy relationship with the One to whom we pray.

You may already have a pattern for your daily life of prayer that is serving you well. In that case, you may make more limited use of some of the segments of this design of a pattern for daily prayer. However, if you do not have such a pattern, I encourage you to try the pattern of prayer offered here. Over a period of several months of daily use, you will adapt and adjust it to your own particular needs that will permit it to become your own personal pattern of prayer.

Do not use it as a rule that must be followed to the letter of the law, rather use it as a guide to daily bring you to awareness of God's presence and the table of rich resources provided for your spiritual nourishment and direction. The movements of the Lord's Prayer and the elements of this pattern of prayer for daily use are important, if not essential, to discovering and practicing our own way of living with God. Becoming aware of God's presence, inviting God's intervention, listening for God's voice, making our requests known, offering ourselves to God, and receiving God's blessing are all essential elements in a faithful and fulfilling life with God. Our task is to weave them into the seamless garment of relationship with God that will sustain us in every experience of life and make it possible for us to live at home with God in this world and the next.

Explanation of the Weekly Readings

The following paragraphs will introduce you to each of the segments of the resource and how they may be used by individuals, families, or small groups. Because we are each different and God is infinite we should not expect our patterns of prayer to be identical. The important part is to establish a daily pattern of prayer that meets your own personal needs and the needs of your family, small group, or larger community and remains faithful to the prayer that Jesus taught us to use.

In a letter to John Trembath, John Wesley said, "O begin! Fix some part of every day for private exercises. You may acquire the taste which you have not: What is tedious at first, will afterwards be pleasant. Whether you like it or no, read and pray daily. It is for your life: there is no other way. . . . Do justice to your own soul: give it time and means to grow. Do not starve yourself any longer" (Vol. 12; p. 254). His words continue to be good advice.

Week Number The readings are numbered from 1 to 56. The first reading begins with the first week of the Advent season. The Scriptures are chosen to follow the lectionary and the church year but the readings can be read in any order. If you are following the church year, the dates at the top of the page will help you move through the year week by week.

Theme The theme for each week of the year is drawn from the three-year lectionary (A, B, and C) Scripture readings for Sunday that are found in the material for each week.

Becoming Aware of God's Presence is a brief Scripture passage for reading and meditation as we make room in our mind and heart to hear and respond to the call of God and to recognize and welcome God's presence in our life, family, or small group.

Inviting God's Intervention is also a brief Scripture or quotation inviting God to act in our lives, our family, our small group, the church, and indeed in the whole world.

Listening for God's Voice is a time when we seek to open our lives more fully to what God is saying to us as an individual, family, or small group. We try to open ourselves to hear what the Scripture passage is saying to us and how the message of the Essay and Quotations inform our walk of faithfulness.

Scripture There are three choices for the Sunday Scripture drawn from the common lectionary. A chart (found on pages 236–239) will help you identify which to choose if you are a member of a congregation following the Ecumenical Sunday Lectionary Scripture readings. If so, you will likely hear the same Scripture read as you worship on Sunday as the one you will read for that day in this daily guide. The Scripture readings for Monday through Friday have been selected to support and enhance the theme for the week.

Essay This is a brief essay written by Rueben P. Job just for that week's reflection. You may think of your own life experiences and how they enlighten your understanding of the theme of the week, the Scripture passage of the day, or the essay of the week.

Quotations are chosen from a wide variety of sources to further illuminate the theme of the week and to prepare you for further spiritual reading from resources listed in the bibliography (pages 233–235).

Reflection Time is designed for you to pause and examine what you have heard and ask how it applies to your life situation. You may choose to meditate on the Scripture, on one of the readings, or on your own life experience and ask what God is saying to you through these resources and this time of reflection.

Making Our Requests Known is when we focus our prayers more precisely on specific things, persons, or events. The prayer that Jesus taught us is the model structure for our own prayer life. However, the structure of our prayers or our prayer time is determined more by our relationship to God and our particular needs at the moment than to any imposed structure. At a time of great thanksgiving, joy, pain, grief, question, fulfillment, loneliness, fear, confidence, or faith the state of our mind, heart, body, and spirit will dictate the form and content of our prayers and often times the structure of our prayers as well.

Offering of Self to God is the time when we offer our lives, all we have, are, and hope to become, to God and invite God to do with us what is best with the full confidence that the One who loves us without limit will provide for us and invest our lives in the work of God in good and meaningful ways. It is a "Your Kingdom come, your will be done, and into your hands I commend my spirit" moment.

Blessing is often a Scripture passage reminding us of God's available presence and blessing to us for the day ahead of us.

Jesus was not stranger to the needs and power of prayer. Some of his prayers are recorded in the Gospels and often he sought times of prayer and solitude. The sixth chapter of Mark reports that Jesus and the disciples were so busy they did not even have time to eat. Sound like anything you experience? Well, it was then that Jesus suggested, "Come away to a deserted place all by yourselves and rest a while" (Mark 6:31a). But when they got to the deserted place, the crowds were already there and Jesus saw them as sheep without a shepherd, had compassion on them, began to teach them, and when it grew late instructed the disciples to feed them (verses 33-34). The compassion of Jesus for the crowds is good news to us.

For we do not embark on our life of prayer on our own. Whether we have been growing in our life with God and our pattern of prayer for decades or if we are just beginning, the One who had compassion on the crowds in the deserted places of their lives, today has compassion on you and on me. And today we claim as our own his promise to the first disciples, "But the Advocate, the Holy Spirit, whom the Father will send in my name, will teach you everything, and remind you of all that I have said to you" (John 14:26).

And so we offer ourselves into the hands of God, ready to be taught, led, formed, and transformed as we daily turn our lives more fully toward God and listen and respond as we are taught and nurtured by the Holy Spirit. May the use of these practices for prayerful living bring new joy, peace, assurance, direction, awareness of God's presence with you, and fulfillment to your life as a follower of Jesus who teaches us how to pray. What more could we ask?

WEEKLY READINGS

Week 1
LOOKING FORWARD

Becoming Aware of God's Presence
Let me hear of your steadfast love in the morning,
    for in you I put my trust. (Psalm 143:8a)

Inviting God's Intervention
Teach me the way I should go,
    for to you I lift up my soul. (Psalm 143:8b)

Listening for God's Voice

Sunday	**A.** Isaiah 2:1-5; Psalm 122; Romans 13:11-14; Matthew 24:36-44
	B. Isaiah 64:1-9; Psalm 80:1-7, 17-19; 1 Corinthians 1:3-9; Mark 13:24-37
	C. Jeremiah 33:14-16; Psalm 25:1-10; 1 Thessalonians 3:9-13; Luke 21:25-36
Monday	Isaiah 1:10-20
Tuesday	1 Thessalonians 1:1-10
Wednesday	Isaiah 2:1-11
Thursday	Isaiah 2:12-22
Friday	Luke 20:41–21:4
Saturday	Luke 21:5-19

Essay
Advent calls us to look forward even when the shadows are long and our vision limited. Of course, there is value in looking back as we remember God's faithfulness in generations gone by and in our own journey of faith. Looking back gives us courage, hope, and trust to look forward with confidence as we watch intently and wait patiently

for the fulfillment of God's promise in our time and our world. What will that fulfillment look like? We do not know the specifics but we do know that it will be a representation of the life and teachings of Jesus. Therefore as we listen again to the promises of God made to Mary and Joseph, we wait with eagerness for God's message to us and pray for grace to respond as faithfully as did they.

Quotations

Today the heart of God is an open wound of love. He aches over our distance and preoccupation. He mourns that we do not draw near to him. He grieves that we have forgotten him. He weeps over our obsession with muchness and manyness. He longs for our presence. And he is inviting you—and me—to come home, to come home to where we belong, to come home to that for which we were created. His arms are stretched out wide to receive us. His heart is enlarged to take us in. (*Prayer: Finding the Heart's True Home*, Richard J. Foster; p. 1.)

Everybody prays. People pray whether or not they call it prayer. We pray every time we ask for help, understanding, or strength, in or out of religion. Then, who, and what we are speak out of us whether we know it or not. Our movements, our stillness, the expressions on our faces, our tone of voice, our actions, what we dream and daydream, as well as what we actually put into words say who and what we are. To pray is to listen to and hear this self who is speaking. This speech is primary because it is basic and fundamental, our ground. In prayer we say who in fact we are—not who we should be, nor who we wish we were, but who we are. All prayer begins with this confession. (*Primary Speech: A Psychology of Prayer*, Ann and Barry Ulanov; p. 1.)

Perhaps the most elusive element in a person's spiritual life is the conviction that he or she is loved, and loved unconditionally, by God. We daily meet many temptations against this truth. Some come from within ourselves, while others find their source in the values of society. (*Free to Pray, Free to Love*, Max Oliva, S. J.; p. 13.)

Every change in the quality of a person's life must grow out of a change in his or her vision of reality. The Christian accepts the Word of Jesus Christ as the master vision of reality. Jesus' Person and teaching shape our understanding of God, the world, other people, and ourselves. This shaping exercises a decisive influence on the Christian's lifestyle. (*The Wisdom of Tenderness*, Brennan Manning; p. 19.)

God's desire for us is that we should live in him. He sends among us the Way to himself. That shows what, in his heart of hearts, God is really like—indeed, what reality is really like. In its deepest nature and meaning our universe is a community of boundless and totally competent love. (*The Divine Conspiracy: Rediscovering Our Hidden Life in God*, Dallas Willard; p. 11.)

"But what good works are those, the practice of which you affirm to be necessary to sanctification?" First, all works of piety; such as public prayer, family prayer, and praying in our closet; receiving the supper of the Lord; searching the Scriptures, by hearing, reading, meditating; and using such a measure of fasting or abstinence as our bodily health allows. (John Wesley, "Sermon 43, The Scripture Way of Salvation," Vol. 6; p. 51.)

Reflection Time

Making Our Requests Known
Prayer for Our World, Its People and Leaders
Prayer for the Church and Its Leaders
Prayer for Those in Our Circle of Responsibility
Prayer for Ourselves

Offering of Self to God

I offer my eyes, ears, and all of my life and invite you to lead me in your way of faithfulness this day and always.

Blessing

Surely God is my salvation;
I will trust, and will not be afraid,
for the LORD GOD is my strength and my might;
he has become my salvation. (Isaiah 12:2)

Week 2

WHERE RIGHTEOUSNESS IS AT HOME

Becoming Aware of God's Presence
But, in accordance with his promise, we wait for new heavens and a new earth, where righteousness is at home. (2 Peter 3:13)

Inviting God's Intervention
Blessed are those who hunger and thirst for righteousness, for they will be filled. (Matthew 5:6)

Listening for God's Voice

Sunday	*A.* Isaiah 11:1-10; Psalm 72:1-7, 18-19; Romans 15:4-13; Matthew 3:1-12
	B. Isaiah 40:1-11; Psalm 85:1-2, 8-13; 2 Peter 3:8-15a; Mark 1:1-8
	C. Malachi 3:1-4; Luke 1:68-79; Philippians 1:3-11; Luke 3:1-6
Monday	Isaiah 61:8-11
Tuesday	2 Corinthians 5:16-21
Wednesday	James 3:13-18
Thursday	Matthew 5:1-11
Friday	Ephesians 4:17-24
Saturday	Psalm 1

Essay
We long for a world where righteousness is at home. It is a world envisioned by the prophets and saints of every age. It is a vision that is reflected in Mary's song and is still the prayer on the lips of the faithful everywhere. We yearn for a world where justice, fairness, equality, goodness, integrity, and well-doing are modeled in industry,

government, school, home, and individual life. Deep in our hearts we know that it is a way of living that will result in a deep sense of well-being and peace for everyone. However, much as we would like to, most of us do not have the wisdom or power to transform the world. But we do have the wisdom and power to permit God to transform us. In our lives, and now and then in the world where we live, righteousness will be at home. You and I can become those persons who carry these gifts of grace to the world.

Quotations

In a Christian believer *love* sits upon the throne which is erected in the inmost soul; namely, love of God and man, which fills the whole heart, and reigns without a rival. In a circle near the throne are all holy tempers;—longsuffering, gentleness, meekness, fidelity, temperance; and if any other were comprised in "the mind which was in Christ Jesus." In an exterior circle are all the *works of mercy*, whether to the souls or bodies of men. (John Wesley, "Sermon 92, On Zeal," Vol. 7; p. 60.)

God's love is *the* foundation of our life. Upon it rests our ultimate identity, our integrity, our hope. It is the good news that sets us free. (*Free to Pray, Free to Love*, Oliva; p. 13.)

Prayer is God's greatest provision for our spiritual life. Our relationship with God is impossible without prayer. We cannot know God's mind or heart without prayer. We cannot receive God's direction, hear God's voice, or respond to God's call without prayer. Since this is true, prayer is also God's greatest provision for all of life. It is the supreme means of grace given to all humankind. Prayer was so very important to Jesus that he left even the needy crowd to pray (Mark 6:31). (*A Wesleyan Spiritual Reader*, Rueben P. Job; p. 16.)

A renewed Christian spirituality will be a spirituality of justice and of peace. It will seek to know and follow God in the pursuit of justice for all people, in the struggle against racism and other forms of domination, in the movement for world peace and nuclear disarmament, and in the campaign against poverty and inequality. In the struggles for a more human world, a renewed spirituality will come to discern the face of God, the holy and just one, and to share the peace of God which passes all understanding. (*The Eye of the Storm*, Kenneth Leech; pp. 230–231.)

Contemplative prayer is the world in which God can do anything. To move into that realm is the greatest adventure. It is to be open to the Infinite and hence to infinite possibilities. Our private, self-made worlds come to an end; a new world appears within and around us and the impossible becomes an everyday experience. (*Open Mind, Open Heart: The Contemplative Dimension of the Gospel*, Thomas Keating; p. 11.)

In mercy and compassion your goodness is revealed;
with tenderness you touch us, and broken hearts are healed.
You claim us as your children, you strip our prideful shame;
with freedom born of mercy we bless your holy name! ("O God Who Shaped Creation." Words: William W. Reid, Jr. Words © 1989 The United Methodist Publishing House.)

Reflection Time

Making Our Requests Known
Prayer for Our World, Its People and Leaders
Prayer for the Church and Its Leaders
Prayer for Those in Our Circle of Responsibility
Prayer for Ourselves

Offering of Self to God
Lead me in paths of righteousness for I am yours.

Blessing

And now I commend you to God and to the message of his grace, a message that is able to build you up and to give you the inheritance among all who are sanctified. (Acts 20:32)

Week 3
WHO ARE YOU LOOKING FOR?

Becoming Aware of God's Presence
Those who are well have no need of a physician, but those who are sick; I have come to call not the righteous but sinners to repentance. (Luke 5:31-32)

Inviting God's Intervention
After this he went out and saw a tax collector named Levi, sitting at the tax booth; and he said to him, "Follow me." (Luke 5:27)

Listening for God's Voice

Sunday	*A.* Isaiah 35:1-10; Psalm 146:5-10; James 5:7-10; Matthew 11:2-11
	B. Isaiah 61:1-4, 8-11; Luke 1:46b-55; 1 Thessalonians 5:16-24; John 1:6-8, 19-28
	C. Zephaniah 3:14-20; Isaiah 12:2-6; Philippians 4:4-7; Luke 3:7-18
Monday	Hebrews 12:1-2
Tuesday	Isaiah 56:1-8
Wednesday	Isaiah 7:10-14
Thursday	Isaiah 52:7-12
Friday	Matthew 2:1-6
Saturday	Luke 1:26-38

Essay
Who are you looking for this Advent season? A break from the routine days of autumn or just a few minutes of escape from the noise of those telling us what we should buy, eat, or do this holiday season? Our preparation for Christmas is often so packed with things to do that we have little time or energy to invest in reflection on what God

may reveal to us in this holy season. I imagine life in the time of Mary and Joseph was much less commercialized but also very busy making a living and planning and preparing for the future.

The angel's announcement of the coming conception of Jesus was a surprise to Mary and we can understand why. The angel's announcement of the birth of a Savior also came as a surprise to the shepherds who were just fulfilling their vocation when suddenly they were drawn in a radically different direction.

What are the messengers (angels) of God saying to you this Advent season? Are you looking for the promised Savior?

Quotations

To pray is to change. This is a great grace. How good of God to provide a path whereby our lives can be taken over by love and joy and peace and patience and kindness and goodness and faithfulness and gentleness and self-control. The movement inward comes first because without interior transformation the movement up into God's glory would overwhelm us and the movement out into ministry would destroy us. (*Prayer*, Foster; p. 6.)

In his passion to set right a disjointed universe, God broke open his own heart of love. The Father sent, not simply a representative, spokesman, or plenipotentiary, but his own Son into the dysfunction of the world so that he might gather that world into the bliss of divine life. God's center—the love between the Father and the Son—is now offered as our center; God's heart breaks open so as to include even the worst and most hopeless among us. (*The Strangest Way: Walking the Christian Path*, Robert Barron; p. 31.)

In his inaugural speech in the Gospel of Mark, Jesus tells the people that God's kingdom is among them, and then he calls them to *metanoia*, to a radical change of mind, body, heart, and soul. What he is saying is this: God's love is now available unconditionally and without restriction, but you must change your whole life if you are to receive it. (*The Strangest Way*, Barron; p. 33.)

The people of God are always on the way to the promised land. To be a follower of Jesus is to be a pilgrim, and it is to be on a journey that always leads us toward God's goodness. The Scriptures remind us that God loves us and seeks to sustain us in all of life. Therefore we can ask for guidance in the confidence that God's way, the very best way, will be made known to us. The vision of the promised land comes from God. The direction and strength to get there also come from God. But if we are to see the vision and to make the journey, we must be willing to give up what we have for that which is not yet fully realized. We need a willingness and openness to discern, to see God's way and, finally, a yearning to be led in that way alone. (*A Guide to Spiritual Discernment*, Rueben P. Job; p. 16.)

From the very beginning Wesley was clear about the sovereignty of God. He never doubted God's ability to care for and provide for all that God had created. God was omnipotent and there could never be any threat to God's power. Wesley did not minimize human responsibility but was always clear that God was sovereign and absolutely no worthy human endeavor could occur without God's participation. If God were to withhold participation, the creation itself would collapse. (*A Wesleyan Spiritual Reader*, Job; p. 43.)

Reflection Time

Making Our Requests Known
Prayer for Our World, Its People and Leaders
Prayer for the Church and Its Leaders
Prayer for Those in Our Circle of Responsibility
Prayer for Ourselves

Offering of Self to God

Help me this day to see you at work in the world around me and to sense your forming of my life more and more in the image you have in mind for me.

Blessing

The LORD will keep you from all evil;
    he will keep your life.
The LORD will keep
    your going out and your coming in
    from this time on and forevermore. (Psalm 121:7-8)

Week 4
HERE I AM

Becoming Aware of God's Presence
Greetings, favored one! The Lord is with you. (Luke 1:28)

Inviting God's Intervention
Here am I, the servant of the Lord; let it be with me according to your word. (Luke 1:38)

Listening for God's Voice

Sunday	*A.* Isaiah 7:10-16; Psalm 80:1-7, 17-19; Romans 1:1-7; Matthew 1:18-25
	B. 2 Samuel 7:1-11, 16; Luke 1:46b-55; Romans 16:25-27; Luke 1:26-38
	C. Micah 5:2-5a; Luke 1:46b-55; Hebrews 10:5-10; Luke 1:39-45, (46-55)
Monday	Isaiah 6:1-8
Tuesday	Jeremiah 1:4-9
Wednesday	Jeremiah 32:16-25
Thursday	1 Samuel 3:1-10
Friday	Colossians 3:1-10
Saturday	Acts 9:10-19

Essay
The congregation where I worship always begins the early morning service with this prayer: "Holy God, help us to be present in worship this day, even as you are present. Amen." I confess that I need that prayer every day!

It is so very hard to live in the present moment, even to be present to God. Our minds dart off in a dozen directions and our focus on God vanishes with the suddenness of a switched-off light. I call my self back, but before I know it the fears of tomorrow or the regrets of yesterday grab my attention; and once again my prayer becomes a plea for help just to stay aware of God's presence and to hold myself there.

Mary's world was surely as turbulent as ours, and the future must have looked grim and foreboding. And yet she brings this total offering of herself to God and to whatever God has in store for her. She is a model for our time of one who demonstrated complete trust in God when the world around her seemed to be gripped by fear and uncertainty. Perhaps she found this deep trust in God because she practiced walking in God's presence every day. Can we remind each other that we too walk in God's presence every day?

Quotations

Joy does not come from positive predictions about the state of the world. It does not depend on the ups and downs of the circumstances of our lives. Joy is based on spiritual knowledge that, while the world in which we live is shrouded in darkness, God has overcome the world. Jesus says it loudly and clearly: "In the world you will have troubles, but rejoice I have overcome the world." The surprise is not that, unexpectedly, things turn out better than expected. No, the real surprise is that God's light is more real than all the darkness, that God's truth is more powerful than all human lies, that God's love is stronger than death. (*Here and Now*, Henri J. M. Nouwen; pp. 36–37.)

In a moment of naked honesty, ask yourself, "Do I wholeheartedly trust that God likes me?" (Not loves me, because theologically God can't do otherwise.) "And do I trust that God likes me, not after I clean up my act and eliminate every trace of sin, selfishness, dishonesty, and degraded love; not after I develop a disciplined prayer life and spend ten years in Calcutta with Mother Teresa's missionaries; but in this moment, right now, right here, with all my faults and weaknesses?" If you answer without hesitation, "Oh yes, God does like me; in fact, he's very fond of me," you're living in the wisdom of accepted tenderness. (*The Wisdom of Tenderness*, Manning; p. 17.)

I want to make a brief notation once again about the particular relevance of quiet morning prayer for those of us who seek to be a caring presence to others. To be involved with God the first thing each day centers us on what is important. In addition, it helps us to awake to the day stretching out before us, one which may be our last. . . . morning silence and solitude can enable us to better come to our senses and be in the now. . . . it is the quiet prayerful space of the early morning that enables us to be better attuned to God's particular call for us each day. Without such an intentional space for prayer, hearing the "voice" of God becomes quite difficult. (*Touching the Holy: Ordinariness, Self-Esteem, and Friendship*, Robert J. Wicks; p. 163.)

Let Jesus use you without consulting you. We let Him take what He wants from us. So take whatever He gives and give whatever He takes with a big smile. Accept the gifts of God and be deeply grateful. If He has given you great wealth, make use of it, try to share it with others, with those who don't have anything. Always share with others because even with a little help you may save them from becoming distressed. And don't take more than you need, that's all. Just accept whatever comes. (*A Simple Path*, Mother Teresa; p. 45.)

Reflection Time

Making Our Requests Known
Prayer for Our World, Its People and Leaders
Prayer for the Church and Its Leaders
Prayer for Those in Our Circle of Responsibility
Prayer for Ourselves

Offering of Self to God

Let me be your servant, under your command.

I will no longer be my own.

I will give up myself to your will in all things. (From "Wesley's Covenant Service," in *The United Methodist Book of Worship* [The United Methodist Publishing House, 1992]; p. 291.)

Blessing

The LORD is faithful in all his words,
  and gracious in all his deeds.
The LORD upholds all who are falling,
  and raises up all who are bowed down. . . .
The LORD is near to all who call on him,
  to all who call on him in truth. (Psalm 145:13b-14, 18)

Week 5

ALARMING THREATS AND FAITHFUL RESPONSE

Becoming Aware of God's Presence

Open to me the gates of righteousness
    that I may enter through them
    and give thanks to the LORD.

This is the gate of the LORD;
    the righteous shall enter through it. (Psalm 118:19-20)

Inviting God's Intervention

Hear my prayer, O LORD;
    let my cry come to you.
Do not hide your face from me
    in the day of my distress.
Incline your ear to me;
    answer me speedily in the day when I call. (Psalm 102:1-2)

Listening for God's Voice

Sunday	**A.** Isaiah 63:7-9; Psalm 148; Hebrews 2:10-18; Matthew 2:13-23
	B. Isaiah 61:10–62:3; Psalm 148; Galatians 4:4-7; Luke 2:22-40*
	C. 1 Samuel 2:18-20, 26; Psalm 148; Colossians 3:12-17; Luke 2:41-52
Monday	Isaiah 12
Tuesday	John 7:37-39
Wednesday	2 Thessalonians 1:1-4
Thursday	Acts 5:27-32

| *Friday* | Acts 9:10-19 |
| *Saturday* | Acts 10:34-43 |

Essay

Our first child was born while we were living in a Chicago suburb. She was healthy, strong, and a delight as we watched her grow and develop. And then suddenly at nine months of age she developed a lung infection that the usual antibiotic could not overcome. Our doctor and pastor were with us when we were told she had a fifty/fifty chance of survival and our only hope was to take a specimen to a Chicago lab to see if an antibiotic could be found that would overcome the infection. With hearts filled with uncertainty and fear we agreed that regardless of the cost the specimen should be taken to the lab. The good news is that in a matter of hours the report came back that there was an antibiotic that could overcome the infection, and a short time later it was delivered to the hospital and given to our daughter.

When a child is threatened we immediately want to act to protect and save the child at all costs. The decision that Joseph and Mary made to follow the guidance of God's messenger meant great hardship but it also meant sparing the life of the child.

What are the threats that you feel for yourself, those you love, the children of the world? What is a faithful response in each situation? We do not know in advance, but we do know the One who can guide us to faithful response no matter the nature or size of the threat.

Quotations

Discernment at its best is the consequence of a daily and lifetime walk with God. A lifetime of such companionship produces profound results that range from guidance in decision making to transformation of one's life. Living a life of discernment, then, is a simple process of staying attentive to and open to God in all of the active and contemplative times of our lives. (*A Guide to Spiritual Discernment*, Job; p. 82.)

There is probably nothing more truly radical than real persons of prayer because they are beholden to no ideology or economic system, but only to God. Both church and state are honestly threatened by true mystics. They can't be bought off because their rewards are elsewhere. (*Everything Belongs*, Richard Rohr; pp. 133–134.)

Our culture says that ruthless competition is the key to success. Jesus says that ruthless compassion is the purpose of our journey. (*Ruthless Trust: The Ragamuffin's Path to God*, Brennan Manning; p. 169.)

There are three ways we can see the whole, and each goes with a particular way of responding to life. First, we can see reality as hostile and threatening. . . . life is filled with threats to our existence: accidents, disease, violence, unemployment, poverty. Life easily looks threatening. . . . If we do see reality this way, how will we respond to life? In a word, defensively. . . . In the second way of seeing the whole, it is perceived as indifferent. . . . If we see reality this way, our response to life will be less anxious . . . but we are still likely to be defensive and precautionary. . . . The third way we can see "what is" is to view it as life-giving and nourishing. It has brought us and everything that is into existence. It sustains our lives. It is filled with wonder and beauty. . . . this is seeing reality as gracious. . . . This way of seeing the whole makes possible a different response to life. It leads to radical trust. It frees us from anxiety, self-preoccupation, and concern to protect the self with systems of security. (*The Heart of Christianity: Rediscovering a Life of Faith*, Marcus J. Borg; pp. 34–35.)

Reflection Time

Making Our Requests Known
Prayer for Our World, Its People and Leaders
Prayer for the Church and Its Leaders
Prayer for Those in Our Circle of Responsibility
Prayer for Ourselves

Offering of Self to God

But as for me, I will look to the LORD,
    I will wait for the God of my salvation;
    my God will hear me. (Micah 7:7)

Blessing

The LORD is my light and my salvation;
    whom shall I fear?
The LORD is the stronghold of my life;
    of whom shall I be afraid? (Psalm 27:1)

*When this date falls on Christmas Day, the following readings may be preferred: Isaiah 52:7-10; Psalm 98; Hebrews 1:1-4, (5-12); John 1:1-14

Week 6
WAITING FOR THE LIGHT

Epiphany Sunday

Becoming Aware of God's Presence
My presence will go with you, and I will give you rest. (Exodus 33:14)

Inviting God's Intervention
Now if I have found favor in your sight, show me your ways, so that I may know you and find favor in your sight. (Exodus 33:13)

Listening for God's Voice

Sunday	*A. B.* and *C.* Isaiah 60:1-6; Psalm 72:1-7, 10-14; Ephesians 3:1-12; Matthew 2:1-12
Monday	Isaiah 42:1-9
Tuesday	Psalm 119:97-105
Wednesday	John 1:1-5
Thursday	Acts 26:19-23
Friday	Matthew 5:14-16
Saturday	1 Peter 2:9-10

Essay
The gift of a robust and vibrant faith is not given easily or often. We may not experience the dark night of the soul that St. John of the Cross experienced, endured, and with which he wrestled until he found some joy and peace as the darkness yielded truth and light. But most of us at some point in our lives experience a sense of abandonment, unworthiness, aloneness that is as palpable in its sorrow as we want the presence of God to be joyful for us. Epiphany assures us that the light is coming and the darkness of confusion, illness,

sinfulness, doubt, and violence that grip our world and darken our world, will not last. As Martin Luther King, Jr., said in the darkest days of the struggle for racial justice, "Darkness cannot drive out darkness: only light can do that" (*A Testament of Hope*; p. 594). So we wait, we endure, we watch, we pray, and we trust that one day the light will come and the darkness will be no more.

Quotations

Let us keep staunch in our eagerness to do whatever comes to us of the truth. Then there will be knocks on our door, over and over, and God's coming will not be hidden. For devoted hearts the light will keep dawning from him who is merciful and compassionate. (From "Action in Waiting," Christoph Friedrich Blumhardt, in *Watch for the Light*; p. 12.)

After a while secularism is boring. It's a dead-end vision; the universe is not enchanted. The bush doesn't burn; it's just a shrub. American culture wants to break out of secularism. Materialism doesn't name our reality adequately. . . . It's like the soul is saying, "There is something more." *The spiritual world is hidden and perfectly revealed in the physical world.* That is the Christ Icon. That's why Jesus is so important; he makes visible the hiding place of God. His body is the revelation of the essential mystery. The material world is the hiding place of God. If we get it in Jesus, we get it. God is perfectly hidden, but once the scales have been taken from our eyes, God is also perfectly revealed and you see the divine image in all material things. If we don't put that together, we will continue to pollute the earth, exhibit unhealthy sexuality, and probably hate ourselves. (*Everything Belongs*, Rohr; pp. 99–100.)

A philosopher of ancient times, Epictetus, once said: "You are a principal work, a fragment of God himself, you have in yourself a part of him. Why then are you ignorant of your high birth?" (*Touching the Holy*, Wicks; p. 79.)

The twentieth-century German-Catholic theologian Karl Adam declared that we believers "start at the top." We don't stand at the bottom of the holy mountain wondering whether we can clamber our way to the summit, attaining the divine through our heroic efforts. On the contrary, through God's grace, we start on the mountaintop, as the beloved children of God, cherished and redeemed. We practice this truth in Jesus' great prayer—beginning, not with supplication and self-deprecation, but with the bold claiming of God as our Father. (*The Strangest Way*, Barron; p. 32.)

So according to the New Testament the dream of a liberator, and the dream of peace, is not merely a dream. The liberator is already present and his power already among us. We can follow him, even today making visible something of the peace, liberty, and righteousness of the kingdom that he will complete. It is no longer impossible. It has become possible for us in fellowship with him. Let us share in his new creation of the world and—born again to a living hope—live as new men and women. (From "The Disarming Child," Jürgen Moltmann, in *Watch for the Light*; p. 323.)

Reflection Time

Making Our Requests Known
Prayer for Our World, Its People and Leaders
Prayer for the Church and Its Leaders
Prayer for Those in Our Circle of Responsibility
Prayer for Ourselves

Offering of Self to God
I give myself to you in confidence and trust, use me as you will for I am yours.

Blessing
It is I who answer and look after you.
I am like an evergreen cypress;

your faithfulness comes from me.
Those who are wise understand these things;
    those who are discerning know them.
For the ways of the LORD are right,
    and the upright walk in them,
    but transgressors stumble in them. (Hosea 14:8b-9)

Week 7
WHEN GOD GETS OUR ATTENTION

Becoming Aware of God's Presence
One afternoon at about three o'clock he had a vision in which he clearly saw an angel of God coming in and saying to him, "Cornelius." (Acts 10:3)

Inviting God's Intervention
While Peter was still thinking about the vision, the Spirit said to him, ". . . Now get up, go down, and go with them without hesitation; for I have sent them." (Acts 10:19-20)

Listening for God's Voice

Sunday	*A.* Isaiah 42:1-9; Psalm 29; Acts 10:34-43; Matthew 3:13-17
	B. Genesis 1:1-5; Psalm 29; Acts 19:1-7; Mark 1:4-11
	C. Isaiah 43:1-7; Psalm 29; Acts 8:14-17; Luke 3:15-17, 21-22
Monday	John 1:29-34
Tuesday	John 1:43-51
Wednesday	Luke 8:19-21
Thursday	Luke 8:22-25
Friday	Mark 2:13-17
Saturday	Mark 6:53-56

Essay
Like a sharp clap of thunder God can get our attention. But at other times God gets our attention with something that may be more like a gentle breeze touching our cheek, or a simple thought or urge that will not let us go. At the baptism of Jesus a voice from heaven got the

attention of those gathered to see the event. However, it was not so much the voice from heaven but the message that got the attention of everyone. The Son of God, the Beloved, with whom God is well pleased, was a message that got everyone's attention. Our task is to listen and pay attention so that we do not miss the gentle whisper or that sharp clap of thunder. They often come unannounced and from many sources, such as Scripture, prayer, worship, events of the day, and other totally unexpected sources. God's presence, power, direction, love, and companionship are continually being revealed.

Quotations

The key to this home, this heart of God, is prayer. Perhaps you have never prayed before except in anguish or terror. It may be that the only time the Divine Name has been on your lips has been in angry expletives. Never mind. I am here to tell you that the Father's heart is open wide—you are welcome to come in. (*Prayer*, Foster; p. 2.)

A life with God is a life in which the rhythms of silence and listening alternate with the rhythms of sharing and service. By praying with every part of who we are, we allow the grace that pours from the well of living water to trickle through all aspects of our being, nourishing and hydrating that which was parched and dis-eased. (*Creating a Life With God*, Daniel Wolpert; p. 159.)

One excellent method of maintaining inward calmness and freedom is to keep putting aside all useless reflections on the past, whether of regret or self-satisfaction. When one duty is accomplished, go steadily on with the next, confining your attention entirely to the one thing God gives you to do, and not putting off difficulties for the future any more than dwelling on regrets for the past. Again, accustom yourself to make frequent brief acts of God's presence through the day amid all your activities. Whenever you are conscious that anxiety or disturbance are springing up within, calm yourself in this way: Cut yourself off from all that is not of God. (*The Royal Way of the Cross*, François Fénelon; p. 127.)

Holy Spirit, Truth divine, dawn upon this soul of mine; Word of God and
inward light, wake my spirit, clear my sight.

Holy Spirit, Love divine, glow within this heart of mine; kindle every
high desire; perish self in thy pure fire;

Holy Spirit, Power divine, fill and
nerve this will of mine; grant that I may
strongly live, bravely bear, and nobly strive.

Holy Spirit, Right divine, King with-
in my conscience reign; be my Lord, and
I shall be firmly bound, forever free. ("Holy Spirit, Truth Divine."
Words: Samuel Longfellow.)

God waits for us and for the ripening of our spirits to enter into this
inheritance. The liturgy is there like Jacob sleeping and dreaming.
When he awoke, he recognized that "this is the gate of heaven." [Gen.
28:16-17] The Spirit of God works in this patterned action with
words and holy things. God waits for us week in and week out in the
here-and now gatherings of the people around tangible items like
water, bread, wine, oil, touch, the play of light, and the arrangement
of space hallowed by prayer. (*Patterned by Grace*, Daniel T. Benedict, Jr.; p. 24.)

Reflection Time

Making Our Requests Known
Prayer for Our World, Its People and Leaders
Prayer for the Church and Its Leaders
Prayer for Those in Our Circle of Responsibility
Prayer for Ourselves

Offering of Self to God

Give me grace to listen for and hear your voice, for I am yours and desire to follow you alone.

Blessing

"I will never leave you or forsake you." So we can say with confidence, "The Lord is my helper;

I will not be afraid.

What can anyone do to me?" (Hebrews 13:5-6)

Week 8
COME AND SEE

Becoming Aware of God's Presence

The LORD is near to all who call on him,
    to all who call on him in truth. (Psalm 145:18)

Inviting God's Intervention

Let my cry come before you, O LORD;
    give me understanding according to your word. (Psalm 119:169)

Listening for God's Voice

Sunday	*A.* Isaiah 49:1-7; Psalm 40:1-11; 1 Corinthians 1:1-9; John 1:29-42
	B. 1 Samuel 3:1-10, (11-20); Psalm 139:1-6, 13-18; 1 Corinthians 6:12-20; John 1:43-51
	C. Isaiah 62:1-5; Psalm 36:5-10; 1 Corinthians 12:1-11; John 2:1-11
Monday	John 14:27-30
Tuesday	Luke 7:36-50
Wednesday	John 14:8-14
Thursday	Acts 17:1-9
Friday	Matthew 12:15-21
Saturday	Luke 9:46-48

Essay

Often our image and understanding of God is far too small. When Nathaniel first heard of Jesus he was skeptical about anything good coming out of Nazareth. Philip responded by inviting him to come and see Jesus for himself. Firsthand experience always trumps what others may say about God and most other things as well. The writer of Colossians says that Jesus is the "image of the invisible God, the firstborn of all creation; for in him all things in heaven and on earth were created . . ." (1:15-26). The first disciples had little to go on but the word of a friend until they began to hang out with Jesus themselves. Then they discovered that Jesus was the real thing. He really was more than just a good man and finally they were able to identify him as Messiah and Son of God. This week we face a few honest questions that the disciples raised about who Jesus really was. Do we know who Jesus is? May we have the courage to face our own questions and to do as those early disciples did, give ourselves to living close enough to Jesus to really get to know who he is and who God is as he gives a clear picture of the relationship between his beloved Abba and himself.

Quotations

That Jesus stood in the Jewish tradition of Spirit-filled mediators is the most important fact for understanding his historical career. His immediate predecessor in this tradition was John the Baptist, and it is a testament to John's spiritual power that it was his baptismal initiation of Jesus that opened Jesus's "third" or spiritual eye, through which he saw the heavens open and the Spirit of God descending upon him like a dove. (*The Soul of Christianity*, Huston Smith; p. 41.)

The people who heard Jesus's disciples proclaiming the Good News were as impressed by what they saw as by what they heard. They saw lives that had been transformed—men and women who were ordinary in every way except for the fact that they seemed to have found the secret of living. They evinced a tranquility, simplicity, and cheerfulness that their hearers had nowhere else encountered. Here were people who seemed to be making a success of the enterprise everyone would like to succeed at—life itself. (*The Soul of Christianity*, Smith; p. 78.)

The greatest gift I have ever received from Jesus Christ has been the Abba experience. "No one knows the Son except the Father, just as no one knows the Father except the Son and those to whom the Son chooses to reveal him" (Matthew 11:27). My dignity as Abba's child is my most coherent sense of self. When I seek to fashion a self-image from the adulation of others and the inner voice whispers, "You've arrived; you're a player in the Kingdom enterprise," there is no truth in that self-concept. When I sink into despondency and the inner voice whispers, "You are a no good fraud, a hypocrite, and a dilettante," there is no truth in any image shaped from that message. (*Abba's Child*, Brennan Manning; p. 62.)

A student of mine shared that he believed that all prayer begins with God. This was a totally new idea for me. I had always held the belief that prayer was up to me. I had to initiate the communication; I had to go to God; I had to get God's attention. Considering that God was the initiator of the prayer relationship turned everything upside down. God was already present. God was waiting for me to respond to God's invitation. All I had to do was say yes. (*A Praying Congregation*, Jane E. Vennard; p. 37.)

In our day we would do everything we could to elevate Jesus to the status of a superstar; in fact, many today try to do this two thousand years after his death on earth. . . . Yet the Gospel record shows that Jesus acted counter to this impulse. Jesus told everyone not to say anything about him. . . . In short, he encouraged others to focus only on God, and in this renunciation, "taking the form of a slave" (Phil. 2:7), he was elevated to become revealed as God, as the greatest of all spiritual leaders. (*Leading a Life With God*, Daniel Wolpert; p. 65.)

Reflection Time

Making Our Requests Known
Prayer for Our World, Its People and Leaders
Prayer for the Church and Its Leaders
Prayer for Those in Our Circle of Responsibility
Prayer for Ourselves

Offering of Self to God

O God, you are my God, I seek you,
    my soul thirsts for you:
my flesh faints for you,
    as in a dry and weary land where there is no water. (Psalm 63:1)

Blessing

May God be gracious to us and bless us
    and make his face to shine upon us,
that your way may be known upon earth,
    your saving power among all nations. (Psalm 67:1-2)

Week 9
FOLLOW ME

Becoming Aware of God's Presence

For the LORD God is a sun and a shield;
  he bestows favor and honor.
No good thing does the LORD withhold
  from those who walk uprightly.
O LORD of hosts,
  happy is everyone who trusts in you. (Psalm 84:11-12)

Inviting God's Intervention

Be merciful to me, O God, be merciful to me,
  for in you my soul takes refuge,
in the shadow of your wings I will take refuge,
  until the destroying storms pass by. (Psalm 57:1)

Listening for God's Voice

Sunday	*A.* Isaiah 9:1-4; Psalm 27:1, 4-9; 1 Corinthians 1:10-18; Matthew 4:12-23
	B. Jonah 3:1-5, 10; Psalm 62:5-12; 1 Corinthians 7:29-31; Mark 1:14-20
	C. Nehemiah 8:1-3, 5-6, 8-10; Psalm 19; 1 Corinthians 12:12-31a; Luke 4:14-21
Monday	Isaiah 6:1-8
Tuesday	Jeremiah 1:4-10
Wednesday	Matthew 10:1-15
Thursday	Acts 1:21-26
Friday	Acts 6:1-6
Saturday	Matthew 14:13-21

Essay

I really like to follow Jesus when he heals the sick, provides food for the hungry, calms my troubled sea, and brings peace to my troubled soul. To see God at work healing my child, providing for the needs of those I love and the whole world makes me feel really good. Who wouldn't want to follow Jesus when we see actions and results like that? But there is more to the story. I am not so sure I would want to be with Jesus when he goes back to his hometown to preach and declares, *"The Spirit of the Lord is upon me, / because he has anointed me / to bring good news to the poor. / He has sent me to proclaim release to the captives / and recovery of sight to the blind, / to let the oppressed go free, / to proclaim the year of the Lord's favor"* (Luke 4:18-19). This message was so unpopular that he was driven out of town by an enraged crowd who didn't like what they heard. I wonder if I could have stood in solidarity with Jesus when the pressure of the culture says his way is all wrong. Yes, I do wonder; but then I remember that he said, *"In the world you face persecution. But take courage; I have conquered the world"* (John 16:33). So by God's grace I take courage today, and with all the faith and trust I can muster, I say *yes* to God's call.

Quotations

The conviction ran deep that because of personal commitment and the power of God at work in a person's life, Christians were to be different. Their goals and priorities were not determined by the culture, or even the church, but by a daily companionship with Jesus Christ. The love of God and neighbor led them to stand against all that was destructive of humankind. The consistent stand against injustice and the untiring efforts to create laws and institutions that brought healing, help, and hope to all people set them apart, often to their peril and pain. No one could follow Jesus Christ and not be identified, and since Methodists were to follow only Christ they were easily recognized. This recognition brought respect as well as derision. But neither counted for anything. The only thing that mattered was faithfulness to God. (*A Wesleyan Spiritual Reader*, Job; p. 193.)

Maybe the real scariness of conversion lies in admitting that God can work in us however, whenever, and through whatever means God chooses. If the incarnation of Jesus Christ teaches us anything, it is that conversion is not one-size-fits-all. Christian conversion is, in fact, incarnational; it is worked out by each individual within the community of faith. I believe that this is what Paul means when asking Christians to conform themselves to Christ. (*Amazing Grace*, Kathleen Norris; p. 42.)

"Follow me." One of the most compelling sentences in the Bible. Two words, when spoken by Jesus, created a sense of power and mystery and awe. To follow is to enter into the unknown, to give your life over to another. We rarely want to do this. Yet at the same time it is exactly what we desire: to be led into a better place, a better world, a better life. This is what Jesus offered to these simple fishermen, and amazingly enough, they took the offer. Their lives would never be the same. (*Leading a Life With God*, Wolpert; p. 116.)

Throughout the Gospels here are two salient aspects of the identity of Jesus. He is from the Father, sent by God to accomplish a task. Secondly, the human journey of Jesus is one that leads back toward God. It is this movement back toward God that is opened to believers of all generations. In following Jesus, we are shown the way that leads toward the Father. Our life is not aimless; it has a destination. We have not been left to wander in the desert; the Shepherd has come to seek what is lost and bring us home. Jesus has gone before us. In the words of John 13:1, he has made the crossing from this world toward the Father and summons us to come after him. (*Toward God: The Ancient Wisdom of Western Prayer*, Michael Casey; p. 2.)

Reflection Time

Making Our Requests Known
Prayer for Our World, Its People and Leaders
Prayer for the Church and Its Leaders

Prayer for Those in Our Circle of Responsibility
Prayer for Ourselves

Offering of Self to God
As you called disciples of old to follow you, so call us today, and grant grace so that we may hear your voice and answer, "Here I am, send me where you will, for I am yours."

Blessing
Therefore the LORD waits to be gracious to you;
   therefore he will rise up to show mercy to you.
For the LORD is a God of justice;
   blessed are all those who wait for him. (Isaiah 30:18)

Week 10
TEACH US HOW TO LIVE

Becoming Aware of God's Presence
You who live in the shelter of the Most High,
   who abide in the shadow of the Almighty,
will say to the LORD, "My refuge and my fortress;
   my God, in whom I trust." (Psalm 91:1-2)

Inviting God's Intervention
Teach me your way, O LORD,
   that I may walk in your truth;
   give me an undivided heart to revere your name.
I give thanks to you, O Lord my God, with my whole heart,
   and I will glorify your name forever. (Psalm 86:11-12)

Listening for God's Voice
Sunday	*A.* Micah 6:1-8; Psalm 15; 1 Corinthians 1:18-31; Matthew 5:1-12
	B. Deuteronomy 18:15-20; Psalm 111; 1 Corinthians 8:1-13; Mark 1:21-28
	C. Jeremiah 1:4-10; Psalm 71:1-6; 1 Corinthians 13:1-13; Luke 4:21-30
Monday	Mark 6:1-13
Tuesday	Luke 11:1-13
Wednesday	Acts 5:33-42
Thursday	Luke 12:1-12
Friday	Psalm 25:1-10
Saturday	Matthew 23:1-12

Essay
When the disciples asked Jesus to teach them how to pray he taught them the prayer that has been our pattern of prayer ever since. In the

Lord's Prayer, Jesus instructed them in prayer, but he did far more than teach the disciples how to pray. He taught them how to live. In Luke's record Jesus reminds the disciples to stay focused, not on their need or on themselves, but on God. Our culture tells us in a thousand ways to stay focused on ourselves and outdo one another by caring for ourselves first. Jesus tells us that the best way to live fully and faithfully is to outdo one another in loving God and neighbor. To follow Jesus is to choose for ourselves the best way to live.

Quotations

Over many years of teaching and writing about prayer, I have become aware that God has given me what I have needed to do this ministry. . . . God's gifts have come through my imagination, as in the times I have suddenly discovered a new image that helps me speak about prayer; they have come through other people with their questions, experiences, and invitations that stretch me into areas of discomfort; and they have come through the love of family, friends, and community who have encouraged and sustained me as my ministry unfolded. God has not granted me a perfect prayer life but an expanding one. There are times when I begin a presentation, wondering how I ever got to this place. That doubt reminds me to breathe a prayer for guidance and to teach about the wonder and mystery of God as best I can. (*A Praying Congregation*, Vennard; p. 97.)

Perfection was a dominant theme in John Wesley's preaching and practice. From the days at Oxford and the Holy Club until his death, he sought a way of living that would lead him closer to God. He wanted to be closer to God and he also wanted to be closer to God's plan for his life. . . . There was a strong yearning for perfection deep within his life and he responded to that yearning by a disciplined life aimed at loving God and neighbor all day every day of his life. Such a disciplined life was not burdensome, but liberating. It was not a morbid affair under an unbearable burden of guilt going on to a destructive self-examination and condemnation. Going on to perfection was a way of living that offered freedom, meaning, and joy. To be moving toward perfection was to be moving toward life at its best. (*A Wesleyan Spiritual Reader*, Job; p. 207.)

In the garden of our souls we are both the farmer and the seed. We've been planted. Our awakening experience has happened. Staying awake is the problem. Our soil soon becomes crowded with weeds. . . . How can we tend the garden of our souls? . . . These monastics were people like you and me. They felt the same impulse we do— they needed help. To find that help, they went to visit the early hermits, quiet dwellers in the desert and asked them, "How do you do it?" "How can I do it?" These wise persons taught them to guard their hearts, to watch their thoughts, to spend time in vigils, to fast, to confess, to practice ceaseless prayer, to practice the prayer of the heart, and to do manual labor, to name a few of the recommended practices. (*Tools Matter for Practicing the Spiritual Life*, Mary Margaret Funk; p. 1.)

We all . . . need to explore together the depths of our popular religious experience. We must probe the hidden places: looking for the signs of eloquence and grace to be found there; listening for deep calling unto deep. . . . And in all of this probing we need to be especially watchful, following Cardinal Newman's advice, for that practical wisdom that dwells "deep in the bosom of the mystical body of Christ." (*Consulting the Faithful*, Richard. J. Mouw; p. 84.)

Reflection Time

Making Our Requests Known
Prayer for Our World, Its People and Leaders
Prayer for the Church and Its Leaders
Prayer for Those in Our Circle of Responsibility
Prayer for Ourselves

Offering of Self to God

Teach me your ways, for I am yours, and my strong desire is to follow you always.

Blessing

They will receive blessing from the LORD,
   and vindication from the God of their salvation.
Such is the company of those who seek him,
   who seek the face of the God of Jacob. (Psalm 24:5-6)

Week 11
THE WAY DISCIPLES LIVE

Becoming Aware of God's Presence
You are a hiding place for me;
> you preserve me from trouble;
> you surround me with glad cries of deliverance. (Psalm 32:7)

Inviting God's Intervention
O guard my life, and deliver me;
> do not let me be put to shame, for I take refuge in you.
May integrity and uprightness preserve me,
> for I wait for you. (Psalm 25:20-21)

Listening for God's Voice

Sunday	*A.* Isaiah 58:1-9a, (9b-12); Psalm 112:1-9, (10); 1 Corinthians 2:1-12, (13-16); Matthew 5:13-20
	B. Isaiah 40:21-31; Psalm 147:1-11, 20c; 1 Corinthians 9:16-23: Mark 1:29-39
	C. Isaiah 6:1-8, (9-13); Psalm 138; 1 Corinthians 15:1-11; Luke 5:1-11
Monday	Luke 9:57-62
Tuesday	Matthew 18:1-5
Wednesday	John 6:60-71
Thursday	Micah 6:6-8
Friday	Luke 12:22-34
Saturday	Luke 10:17-24

Essay
Living with Jesus is not easy. It never was. Even a casual reading of the Gospels shakes us up because they make it clear that living as a disciple brings earthshaking challenges. Jesus was physically with

the first disciples to coach, teach, mentor, encourage, guide, protect, and provide. Still these early disciples were often perplexed, uncertain, and fearful. There were times when they just didn't get it.

The way Jesus plunged across boundaries and accepted everyone where they were was enough to keep them off balance as they tried to understand and keep up with their leader. Of course there were other times when they were filled with exuberance, confidence, courage, integrity, understanding, and strength. Those times when they rose to the challenge of living as a faithful disciple of Jesus.

In our deepest and best moments that is the way we would like to live all the time. But when those complacency-shattering requests come, the ones that shatter our comfortable boundaries, we too get nervous, unsettled, and sometimes very much afraid. The good news is that Jesus still comes to us in the power and presence of the Holy Spirit to help us understand and to give us all the strength we need to prevail as faithful disciples. All we need to do is ask.

Today, when those complacency-shattering requests come that seem impossible to fulfill, Jesus is still with us through the power and presence of the Holy Spirit to offer to us the help we need to live faithfully as a follower of Jesus.

Quotations
Overwork is the biggest obstacle to seekers moving toward the kind of prayer that is absorption into God beyond images. We need an environment that will image back to us all that is or is not of God. This is why a cell is a sacred place that is kept deliberately simple. . . . The cell is really the secret closet that Matthew talks about where we talk to our Father in secret (Matt. 6:6). It's not really a place or a time after awhile, but an act of descending the mind into the heart and dwelling there. All of us need an external mechanism to protect our internal world. (*Tools Matter for Practicing the Spiritual Life*, Funk; pp. 70–71.)

The Prayer of Relinquishment is a bona fide letting go, but it is a release with hope. We have no fatalist resignation. We are buoyed up by a confident trust in the character of God. Even when all we see are tangled threads on the backside of life's tapestry, we know that God is good and is out to do us good always. That gives us hope to believe that we are the winners, regardless of what we are being called upon to relinquish. God is inviting us deeper in and higher up. There is training in righteousness, transforming power, new joys, deeper intimacy. (*Prayer*, Foster; p. 52.)

It is impossible to live in close communion with any person and not take on some of the qualities of that person. So it is with Jesus Christ. To live with Jesus is to begin to take on the qualities that marked his life. Unqualified love for and obedience to God, unconditional love of neighbor, and a radical selflessness were an integral part of the life and ministry of Jesus. To follow Jesus is to incorporate these qualities into our lives as well. (*A Wesleyan Spiritual Reader*, Job; p. 76.)

We must not so stress our relationship with God that we forget our relationship with one another. And we must not so stress our relationship with one another that we have no need to look to God for forgiveness. Reconciliation involves both God and neighbors. Anyone committed to living a life of reconciliation must attend to the dynamics of love in relationship with God, others, self, and the world. (*To Walk Together Again*, Richard M. Gula, S. S.; p. 16.)

When we pray for others, we not only seek something for them but we also acknowledge our dependency on them. We only achieve being through relationships with others, with other real persons. A glimpse of this mystery and its fundamental reality appears in the image of the Trinity. The internal being of God exists as relationship, a love so vital and vividly expressed that only the image of persons in unceasing connection to each other can capture it. Jesus indicates that this sort of interconnectedness both preceded his birth and survives after his death as a principal way to link us to God through him. "He always lives to make intercession for [us]," as the words of Hebrews put it. (Hebrews 7:25) (*Primary Speech*, Ulanov; pp. 85–86.)

Reflection Time

Making Our Requests Known
Prayer for Our World, Its People and Leaders
Prayer for the Church and Its Leaders
Prayer for Those in Our Circle of Responsibility
Prayer for Ourselves

Offering of Self to God
For, as I can testify, they voluntarily gave according to their means, and even beyond their means, begging us earnestly for the privilege of sharing in this ministry to the saints—and this, not merely as we expected; they gave themselves first to the Lord . . . (2 Corinthians 8:3-5)

Blessing
Keep alert, stand firm in your faith, be courageous, be strong. Let all that you do be done in love. (1 Corinthians 16:13-14)

Week 12
IN NEED OF HEALING

Becoming Aware of God's Presence

The heavens are telling the glory of God;
    and the firmament proclaims his handiwork.
Day to day pours forth speech,
    and night to night declares knowledge. (Psalm 19:1-2)

Inviting God's Intervention

Do not, O LORD, withhold
    your mercy from me;
let your steadfast love and your faithfulness
    keep me safe forever. (Psalm 40:11)

Listening for God's Voice

Sunday	*A.* Deuteronomy 30:15-20; Psalm 119:1-8; 1 Corinthians 3:1-9; Matthew 5:21-37
	B. 2 Kings 5:1-14; Psalm 30; 1 Corinthians 9:24-27; Mark 1:40-45
	C. Jeremiah 17:5-10; Psalm 1; 1 Corinthians 15:12-20; Luke 6:17-26
Monday	Matthew 4:23-25
Tuesday	Ephesians 4:25-32
Wednesday	Acts 3:1-10
Thursday	Matthew 8:1-4
Friday	Job 29:1-20
Saturday	Psalm 1

Essay

Sitting in a crowded waiting room of a large university medical center, I was struck by the great variety of persons in the room. Some very old who needed assistance to walk and some very young who were being carried and with nearly every color of skin represented. I assumed the one thing they had in common was that they wanted to be healed of whatever ailment brought them there. Waiting for my name to be called, I thought of the experience of Jesus at the pool in Jerusalem as it is told in John 5:2-9. The "clinic at the pool" was also crowded when Jesus approached and spoke to a man who had been ill for thirty-eight years. It is not surprising that Jesus, who seemed to show compassion to everyone he met, spoke to the person who had been there so long seeking a cure.

The surprising thing is that Jesus asked him if he wanted to be made well. What a silly question. Everyone wants to be made well. This man had been there seeking healing for what must have seemed like a lifetime and in response to the question, "Do you want to be healed?" he replies that he has no one to help him get into the healing water at the right time. Jesus then tells him to "Stand up, take your mat and walk." I wondered what the doctor would tell each of the persons in the waiting room and what she would tell me. How much of my well-being is up to me? What must I do to appropriate God's life-giving power in my life?

Quotations

Healing Prayer is part of the normal Christian life. It should not be elevated above any other ministry in the community of faith, nor should it be undervalued; rather, it should be kept in proper balance. It is simply a normal aspect of what it means to live under the reign of God. This should not surprise us, for it is a clear recognition of the incarnational nature of our faith. God cares as much about the body as he does the soul, as much about the emotions as he does the spirit. The redemption that is in Jesus is total, involving every aspect of the person—body, soul, will, mind, emotions, spirit. (*Prayer*, Foster; p. 203.)

Even when we know that we are called to be wounded healers, it is still very difficult to acknowledge that healing has to take place today. Because we are living in days when our wounds have become all too visible. Our loneliness and isolation has become so much a part of our daily experience, that we cry out for a Liberator who will take us away from our misery and bring us justice and peace. To announce, however, that the Liberator is sitting among the poor and that the wounds are signs of hope and that today is the day of liberation, is a step very few can take. But this is exactly the announcement of the wounded healer: "The Master is coming—not tomorrow, but today, not next year, but this year, not after all our misery is passed, but in the middle of it, not in another place but right here where we are standing." (*The Wounded Healer*, Henri J. M. Nouwen; p. 95.)

God's fullest revelation as love and goodness by nature is made in his incarnate Word, Jesus Christ. For in him we have not only words, but we have the one Word that is the perfect copy of God's nature. In him we can come not only to know God's very nature as a community of mutual, sharing persons, Father, Son, and Holy Spirit, but we can be brought into a loving communion with God's very being through the risen Lord's Spirit. We can become good, not in ourselves, but as true participators in God's very own nature. (*In Jesus We Trust*, George A. Maloney, S. J.; p. 20.)

One of the basic consequences of living as a Christian is coming to know ourselves. That entails both struggle and joy. It is a lifetime task that leads to wholeness not only within ourselves but in our perception of all of the reality that surrounds us. It is this integration that makes it possible for us not only to call Jesus' name, but to accept the consequences. We will be called to submit to the fire and be transformed, to climb mountains and to relax in the cool valley by a refreshing stream. The slopes and the upgrades of our lives will alternate, but we will have the constant reassurance of following one who loves us and knows how to set the pace. (*Symbols of Inner Truth*, Carole Marie Kelly, O. S. F.; p. 48.)

If Christ is born in our hearts, will the world ever feel it? Will government and business, our beloved earth or our disenfranchised masses be affected? We cannot answer that we are not good enough or are not schooled enough or are not recognized. We can only begin where we are. . . . To all those who receive him, who believe in his name, Christ still gives "the power to become the children of God" (John 1:12) and, with this inheritance, his grace to love to life the earth and all its people. (*Faith, the Yes of the Heart*, Grace Adolphsen Brame; p. 92.)

Reflection Time

Making Our Requests Known
Prayer for Our World, Its People and Leaders
Prayer for the Church and Its Leaders
Prayer for Those in Our Circle of Responsibility
Prayer for Ourselves

Offering of Self to God
O Lord, my God, I give to you as much of self as I am able to give this day. Lead me in faithfulness and righteousness until I am whole and wholly yours.

Blessing
This day we claim the promise, presence, and power of God to bring us to our full humanity, whole and happy as God's beloved children.

Week 13

LOOKING FOR THE RIGHT WAY

Becoming Aware of God's Presence

You who live in the shelter of the Most High,
who abide in the shadow of the Almighty,
will say to the LORD, "My refuge and my fortress;
my God, in whom I trust." (Psalm 91:1-2)

Inviting God's Intervention

In you, O LORD, I take refuge;
let me never put to shame.
In your righteousness deliver me and rescue me;
incline your ear to me and save me.
Be to me a rock of refuge,
a strong fortress, to save me,
for you are my rock and my fortress. (Psalm 71:1-3)

Listening for God's Voice

Sunday	*A.* Leviticus 19:1-2, 9-18; Psalm 119:33-40; 1 Corinthians 3:10-11, 16-23; Matthew 5:38-48
	B. Isaiah 43:18-25; Psalm 41; 2 Corinthians 1:18-22; Mark 2:1-12
	C. Genesis 45:3-11, 15; Psalm 37:1-11, 39-40; 1 Corinthians 15:35-38, 42-50; Luke 6:27-38
Monday	Matthew 5:17-20
Tuesday	Romans 8:18-27
Wednesday	Matthew 7:15-20
Thursday	Galatians 5:13-15
Friday	Galatians 5:16-21
Saturday	Galatians 5:22-26

Essay

Why is it that in my eight decades of living I still have to look for the right way? Of course, practicing the right way for a long time does develop excellent habits and right responses to many of life's experiences. But sometimes I still find myself struggling to find the right word, the right answer, the right decision, and the right path. Why? Because I am alive and the world around me is alive and pulsing with questions, invitations, and declarations that are not always aimed at the common good or seek the best for me. And these sometimes subtle and sometimes bold efforts at leading me in a wrong direction nibble away at my resolve and my good habits. Perhaps that is why Jesus said, "And remember, I am with you always . . ." (Matthew 28:20). While the first disciples had their face-to-face, three-year course of study, Jesus promised to be with them always to guide, companion, instruct, and encourage. It is a promise that we claim for ourselves today.

Quotations

The power by which God transforms humans is the Holy Spirit. Christian spirituality is therefore not a matter of cultivating some dimension of the human spirit, but a matter of obedient response to the Spirit of God. (*The Creed*, Luke Timothy Johnson; p. 245.)

If we take seriously the word of the risen Christ, "Know that I am with you always; yes, to the end of time" (Matthew 28:20), we should expect that that He will be actively present in our lives. If our faith is alive and luminous, we will be alert to moments, events, and occasions when the power of resurrection is brought to bear on our lives. Self-absorbed and inattentive, we fail to notice the subtle ways in which Jesus is snagging our attention. William Barry wrote, "we must school ourselves to pay attention to our experience of life in order to discern the touch of God or what Peter Berger calls the *rumor of angels* from all the other influences on our experience." (*Abba's Child*, Manning; pp. 99–100.)

God is present, hoping, and urging, in the midst of all the situations of life. As Christians, we believe that God is passionately involved in human affairs and intimately invested in all our questioning. Moreover, we believe that God's involvement in our lives has purpose and direction. God is seeking to bring healing and wholeness and reconciliation, transforming this broken world into that New Creation where there will be no more sadness or injustice or pain. Our decisions and our search for guidance take place in the active presence of a God who intimately cares about our life situations and who invites us to participate in the divine activities of healing and transformation. (*Practicing Our Faith*, Dorothy C. Bass, ed.; p. 106.)

In modern life we have become so busy with our daily affairs and thoughts that we have forgotten this essential art of taking time to converse with our heart. When we ask it about our current path, we must look at the values we have chosen to live by. Where do we put our time, our strength, our creativity, our love? We must look at our life without sentimentality, exaggeration, or idealism. Does what we are choosing reflect what we most deeply value? (*A Path With Heart*, Jack Kornfield; p. 12.)

The gospel, while honoring our experience, doesn't begin with our experience. We don't begin a holy life by wanting a holy life, desiring to be good, fulfilled, complete, or wanting to be included in the grand scheme of things. We have been anticipated, and the way we have been anticipated is by resurrection, Jesus' resurrection. Living a holy life, the Christian equivalent of revolution, begins with Jesus' resurrection. (*Christ Plays in Ten Thousand Places*, Eugene H. Peterson; p. 230.)

Reflection Time

Making Our Requests Known
Prayer for Our World, Its People and Leaders
Prayer for the Church and Its Leaders

Prayer for Those in Our Circle of Responsibility
Prayer for Ourselves

Offering of Self to God
With gratitude for your constant love and care, Almighty God, I offer myself to you in faith and confidence that you will accept and make whole and perfect all that is given to you.

Blessing
The LORD bless you and keep you;
the LORD make his face to shine
    upon you, and be gracious to you;
the LORD lift up his countenance
    upon you, and give you peace. (Numbers 6:24-26)

Week 14

JESUS AS OUR TEACHER

Becoming Aware of God's Presence

Lord, you have been our dwelling place
    in all generations.
Before the mountains were brought forth
    or ever you had formed the earth and the world,
    from everlasting to everlasting you are God. (Psalm 90:1-2)

Inviting God's Intervention

Teach me to do your will,
    for you are my God.
Let your good spirit lead me
    on a level path. (Psalm 143:10)

Listening for God's Voice

Sunday	*A.* Isaiah 49:8–16a; Psalm 131; 1 Corinthians 4:1–5; Matthew 6:24-34
	B. Hosea 2:14-20; Psalm 103:1-13, 22; 2 Corinthians 3:1-6; Mark 2:13-22
	C. Isaiah 55:10-13; Psalm 92:1-4, 12-15; 1 Corinthians 15:51-58; Luke 6:39-49
Monday	Micah 4:1-5
Tuesday	Luke 4:31-37
Wednesday	Mark 1:21-28
Thursday	John 7:10-24
Friday	Matthew 23:1-12
Saturday	Luke 12:8-12

Essay

Jesus the master teacher surprises us with the easy way he offers earthshaking principles and a revolutionary way of life. For the most part we have tamed those teachings to something we can tolerate without too much embarrassment at our failure to actually practice what Jesus lived and taught. But in our better moments we do want to be like Jesus, live like Jesus, and die like Jesus. Well, maybe we do sometimes, but we like to choose the times and the places.

But upon closer examination we realize that even though Jesus lived a pretty risky life, challenging the religious authority as well as the cultural wisdom of his day, we do want to live like him and be like him. When we sit with and walk with this master teacher we will be taught new ways of living and of being. And if we have the courage to continue in the presence of this master teacher, we may find our lives transformed more and more into that divine image that we all carry deep within, although sometimes hidden behind our fears. May we spend this day in the classroom with Jesus.

Quotations

Now disciples of Jesus are people who want to take into their being the order of The Kingdom Among Us. They wish to live their life in it as Jesus himself would, and that requires internalization of that order. Study is the chief way in which they do it. They devote their attention, their thoughtful inquiry, and their practical experimentation to the order of the kingdom as seen in Jesus, in the written word of Scripture, in others who walk in the way, and, indeed, in every good thing in nature, history, and culture. (*The Divine Conspiracy*, Willard; p. 361.)

While being so busy running my own life, I become oblivious to the gentle movements of the Spirit of God within me, pointing me in directions quite different from my own. . . . God does not shout, scream, or push. The Spirit of God is soft and gentle like a small voice or a light breeze. It is the spirit of love. Maybe we still do not fully believe that God's Spirit is, indeed, the Spirit of love, always leading us deeper into love. Maybe we still distrust the Spirit, afraid to be led to places where our freedom is taken away. Maybe we still think of God's Spirit as an enemy who wants something of us that is not good for us. But God is love, and only love, and God's Spirit is the Spirit of love longing to guide us to the place where the deepest desires of our hearts can be fulfilled. (*Here and Now*, Nouwen; pp. 58–59.)

For the most part we do not become fluent in the language of prayer on our own, or by reading a book, or by signing up for a course. We become fluent in prayer by keeping company with Jesus. We learn to pray "in Jesus' name." (*Tell It Slant*, Eugene H. Peterson; p. 267.)

In his last, never-to-be-forgotten evening with his friends, Jesus did what so many do when they are about to die. He spoke of what mattered most. He told his friends that he loved them. He asked that they take care of each other for his sake. Then he added something vitally important; "Abide in me as I abide in you. . . . Apart from me you can do nothing" (John 15:4-5). What did he mean? Abiding is dwelling, living in God: a constant connection, a continuing communion based on complete trust. Jesus was going away bodily, but his Spirit would remain, abiding with those he loved. He invited his followers to reciprocate, to depend on him and on the one who sent him. (*Faith, the Yes of the Heart*, Brame; p. 96.)

Reflection Time

Making Our Requests Known
Prayer for Our World, Its People and Leaders
Prayer for the Church and Its Leaders
Prayer for Those in Our Circle of Responsibility
Prayer for Ourselves

Offering of Self to God

Trusting in your love, wisdom, mercy, and power, I give myself to you and invite you to always fulfill your purpose in my life.

Blessing

May the Holy Spirit teach, guide, companion, and comfort you this day and always.

Week 15
LISTENING TO JESUS

Becoming Aware of God's Presence
Then from the cloud came a voice that said, "This is my Son, my Chosen; listen to him!" (Luke 9:35)

Inviting God's Intervention
Loving teacher, help us to open our minds, hearts, and entire lives to you. Come, speak to us, teach us, lead us, and form us until we are more and more like you; for we are yours.

Listening for God's Voice

Sunday	*A.* Exodus 24:12-18; Psalm 2; 2 Peter 1:16-21; Matthew 17:1-9
	B. 2 Kings 2:1-12; Psalm 50:1-6; 2 Corinthians 4:3-6; Mark 9:2-9
	C. Exodus 34:29-35; Psalm 99; 2 Corinthians 3:12–4:2; Luke 9:28-36, (37-43)
Monday	Luke 11:27-28
Tuesday	Isaiah 42:1-9
Wednesday	Hebrews 3:7-15
Thursday	John 10:1-6
Friday	Acts 13:44-52
Saturday	Acts 28:23-31

Essay
It is difficult to follow Jesus if we do not know where he is going and where he wants to lead us. The voice from the cloud told those first disciples to listen to Jesus. I imagine the advice is true for us as well. It is so important for us to find ways of listening to what Jesus has to say to us today.

Of course this is true so that we may know what it means to follow Jesus, and it is also true so that we may find grace and strength to do so. We may not be able to open our lives to the amazing grace that is available to guide us, sustain us, comfort us, and keep us unless we listen to hear where Jesus is leading us. So we learn to listen so that we will not miss the most important voice of all time with the most important message we will ever hear.

Quotations

A new beginning! We must learn to live each day, each hour, yes, each minute as a new beginning, as a unique opportunity to make everything new. Imagine that we could live each moment as a moment pregnant with new life. Imagine that we could live each day as a day full of promises. Imagine that we could walk through the new year always listening to a voice saying to us: "I have a gift for you and can't wait for you to see it!" Imagine. . . . we must open our minds and hearts to the voice that resounds through the valleys and hills of our life saying: "Let me show you where I live among my people. My name is 'God-with-you.' I will wipe away all the tears from your eyes; there will be no more death, and no more mourning or sadness. The world of the past has gone" (see Revelation 21:2-5). We must choose to listen to that voice, and every choice will open us a little more to discover new life hidden in the moment, waiting eagerly to be born. (*Here and Now*, Nouwen; pp. 16–17.)

The true prophetic message always calls us to a spiritual defiance of the world as it now is. Our prayer, to the extent that it is fully authentic, undermines the status quo. It is a spiritual underground resistance movement. We are subversive in a world of injustice, oppression, and violence. Like Amos of old, we demand that "justice roll down like waters, and righteousness like an everflowing stream" (Amos 5:24). We plead the case of the orphan and the widow, or whoever the helpless ones are in our context. In our prayers and in our actions we stand firm against racism, sexism, nationalism, ageism, and every other "ism" that separates and splits and divides. (*Prayer*, Foster; p. 247.)

This is the only time in the Gospels that the disciples ask to be taught, the only time that Jesus is addressed by his disciples in the verbal imperative: "teach us." Jesus taught daily. He taught in field and synagogue and temple. The disciples for a considerable time through the Galilean years have observed Jesus praying. Now they ask, "teach us." They have had the introductory courses in living Jesus' way and are now eligible for an upper-level elective. And what do they choose? Prayer. "Teach us to pray." (*Tell It Slant*, Peterson; pp. 47–48.)

In religious circles we find today a fierce and almost violent planning and programming, a sense that without ceaseless activity nothing will ever be accomplished. How seldom it occurs to us that God has to undo and do all over again so much of what we in our willfulness have pushed through in [God's] name. How little there is in us of the silent and radiant strength in which the secret works of God really take place! How ready we are to speak, how loathe to listen, to sense the further dimension of what it is that we confront. (*Dimensions of Prayer*, Douglas V. Steere; pp. 4–5.)

Prayer is the soul's sincere desire, un-
uttered or expressed, the motion of a
hidden fire that trembles in the breast.

Prayer is the simplest form of speech that
infant lips can try; prayer the sublimest
strains that reach the Majesty on high.

O Thou, by whom we come to God, the
Life, the Truth, the Way: the path of prayer thy-
self hast trod; Lord, teach us how to pray! ("Prayer Is the Soul's Sincere Desire." Words: James Montgomery.)

Reflection Time

Making Our Requests Known
Prayer for Our World, Its People and Leaders
Prayer for the Church and Its Leaders
Prayer for Those in Our Circle of Responsibility
Prayer for Ourselves

Offering of Self to God
Because you first loved us and have chosen us, we are bold to offer ourselves to you and we listen for your voice of direction and invite you to work your perfect will in our lives this day and always.

Blessing
Walk this day in Holy presence listening for, hearing, and responding quickly and faithfully to God's slightest whisper in all things.

Week 16
LEARNING WHO WE ARE

Becoming Aware of God's Presence

What then are we to say about these things? If God is for us, who is against us? He who did not withhold his own Son, but gave him up for all of us, will he not with him also give us everything else? (Romans 8:31-32)

Inviting God's Intervention

O LORD, be gracious to us; we wait for you.
Be our arm every morning,
our salvation in the time of trouble. (Isaiah 33:2)

Listening for God's Voice

Sunday	*A.* Genesis 2:15-17; 3:1-7; Psalm 32; Romans 5:12-19; Matthew 4:1-11
	B. Genesis 9:8-17; Psalm 25:1-10; 1 Peter 3:18-22; Mark 1:9-15
	C. Deuteronomy 26:1-11; Psalm 91:1-2, 9-16; Romans 10:8b-13; Luke 4:1-13
Monday	2 Samuel 23:1-4
Tuesday	2 Corinthians 4:1-15
Wednesday	Luke 22:39-46
Thursday	James 1:12-18
Friday	1 Peter 4:12-19
Saturday	1 Peter 5:1-11

Essay

We tend to forget that Jesus was fully human and faced the temptations and questions of life just as we do. Perhaps that is why the

Gospel accounts in each of the three-year cycles of suggested Scripture for this first Sunday in Lent tell of what happened to Jesus immediately after being baptized in the Jordan River by John. There was the affirmation of a voice from heaven declaring, "You are my Son, the Beloved; with you I am well pleased" (Luke 3:22). But then comes the account of the forty days of temptation and trial in the wilderness. These forty days of fasting and prayer with only the companionship of his beloved "Abba" were a time of discovery of self, growing trust in "Abba," and of offering of self without reservation. May our Lenten journeys be as much for each of us.

Quotations

In the first three centuries the training of Christian leaders occurred on the job. . . . [The disciples] learned the significance of prayer or other acts of symbolic devotion, therefore, from seeing them in the life of Jesus, an observant Jew with a strong divine consciousness. If we may trust the impression left by the Synoptic Gospels, Jesus implanted in their minds the necessity of a profound God-awareness in all of life that was to be sharpened by prayer and other acts of worship. (*Spiritual Preparation for Christian Leadership*, E. Glenn Hinson; pp. 15–16.)

Let's return to the biblical scene of Christ's last evening with his disciples in the Garden of Gethsemane. The disciples were full of good intentions, but Jesus understood their condition. In the light of this knowledge he advised a course of action that would enable them to do what he knew they sincerely wanted to do. "Watch and pray," he said, "that ye enter not into temptation; the spirit indeed is willing, but the flesh is weak" (Matt. 24:41). The plain meaning of this advice to his sleepy and worried friends was that by engaging in a certain type of action—the keeping of vigil combined with prayer—they would be able to attain a level of spiritual responsiveness and power in their lives that would be impossible without it. In this simple but profound episode we find the whole nature and principle of the kind of activity that is a spiritual discipline. (*The Spirit of the Disciplines*, Dallas Willard; p. 151.)

"Holiness," said Walter Rauschenbusch, "is goodness on fire." This captures well the holiness—and the danger—of Jesus, his power to attract and disturb . . . before re-creation or redemption can occur. . . . Most of us, along with our culture, create some tamer, more easily contained version of Jesus and the holiness he represents. A Jesus who becomes easy to laugh at, shrug off, dismiss. . . . Not a person, not the living God who speaks and rattles the foundations of the earth. (*Why Jesus Makes Me Nervous*, Joy Jordan-Lake; p. 44.)

From the way Jesus talked about God and enacted the reign of God, it is obvious that he had a special and original experience of God as intimate, close, and tremendously compassionate over human suffering and sin. Out of that experience Jesus surfaced a name for God, namely *Abbe*. In the Hebrew Scriptures God is occasionally called "Father" in some of the psalms and prophets. But *Abbe* does not exactly mean Father. It is the Aramaic word that a small child would use to address his or her father before being able to talk. As such a babble word, it really translates into English as "papa" or "dada" or some other equivalent. Every language has these little words that children use before they can really speak, but which they can use to call on their nearest and dearest. Jesus' own personal experience of God as close and compassionate led him to name God in this very intimate way, *Abbe*. The name evokes the power of a very close relationship between Jesus and the One he names this way. Furthermore, Jesus teaches others to call God *Abbe*, encouraging them to trust God the way little children trust a good parent to take care of them, be compassionate over their weakness, and stand guard against those who would harm them. Jesus' *Abbe* experience is the heart of the matter, the dynamism behind his preaching the reign of God and of his typical way of acting. God *Abbe* was the passion of his life. (*Consider Jesus*, Elizabeth A. Johnson; p. 57.)

Reflection Time

Making Our Requests Known
Prayer for Our World, Its People and Leaders
Prayer for the Church and Its Leaders
Prayer for Those in Our Circle of Responsibility
Prayer for Ourselves

Offering of Self to God
God of love and compassion, author of life and all creation, we now offer ourselves to you and invite your presence fully into our lives to mold and shape us, as a skilled potter brings forth something good, useful, and beautiful from malleable clay.

Blessing
We leave this time of prayer and reflection, remembering who we are as God's children and filled with confidence and peace because God is with us.

Week 17

DISCIPLESHIP IS NOT TOO COSTLY

Becoming Aware of God's Presence

Seek the LORD and his strength;
  seek his presence continually.
Remember the wonderful works he has done,
  his miracles, and the judgments he has uttered . . . (Psalm 105:4-5)

Inviting God's Intervention

With my whole heart I seek you;
  do not let me stray from your commandments.
I treasure your word in my heart,
  so that I may not sin against you.
Blessed are you, O LORD;
  teach me your statutes. (Psalm 119:10-12)

Listening for God's Voice

Sunday	*A.* Genesis 12:1-4a; Psalm 121; Romans 4:1-5, 13-17; John 3:1-17
	B. Genesis 17:1-7, 15-16; Psalm 22:23-31; Romans 4:13-25; Mark 8:31-38
	C. Genesis 15:1-12, 17-18; Psalm 27; Philippians 3:17–4:1; Luke 13:31-35
Monday	Matthew 16:24-28
Tuesday	Luke 14:25-33
Wednesday	Acts 14:19-23
Thursday	Mark 10:28-31
Friday	Acts 28:11-22
Saturday	John 8:31-38

Essay

Following Jesus in a world like ours is not all that easy. There are costs involved. And why would we think otherwise? Living as a radical child of God was not that easy for Jesus, either. And the twelve found the earth moved beneath their feet, too, as they tried to follow not only the teachings of Jesus, but Jesus himself. But they also noticed that those who did not follow Jesus not only felt the earth move beneath their feet, they saw their world come apart. The twelve discovered that the cost of being a disciple was so minimal compared to the benefit of being a disciple that, upon close examination, it was a no-brainer to choose to follow the One who alone could give the gift of constant companionship with the living God in this world and the next. In a world like ours only a life fully given to God can find fulfillment, security, a deep and abiding peace, and the intimate companionship of God. That is exactly where I want to live. How about you?

Quotations

Many are the things of which the believer has need in order to attain knowledge of God and virtue: deliverance from passions, patient acceptance of trials, the inner principles of virtues, . . . in short there are countless other things which help us to reject sin and ignorance and to attain knowledge and virtue. It was surely because of this that the Lord said, "Whatever you ask for in prayer, believing, you will receive" (Matt. 21:22), stating simply that the devout must seek and ask with understanding and faith for all those things, and for those alone, which lead to virtue and knowledge of God. For all these things are profitable, and unquestionably the Lord gives them to those who ask. (*The Philokalia*, Vol. 2, St. Nikodimos of the Holy Mountain and St. Makarios of Corinth; p. 191.)

I do not fully understand the reasons for the wildernesses of God's absence. This I do know: while the wilderness is necessary, it is never meant to be permanent. In God's time and in God's way the desert will give way to a land flowing with milk and honey. And as we wait for that promised land of the soul, we can echo the prayer of Bernard of Clairvaux, "O my God, deep calls unto deep (Ps. 42:7). The deep of my profound misery calls to the deep of Your infinite mercy." (*Prayer*, Foster; p. 24.)

True children of God realize in life's circumstances that we have no strength of our own. In all moments we are to confess our weaknesses to do good by our own efforts. We know with St. Paul that all our strength is to be found in Christ. Our very weakness, when recognized, can become our strength as we lovingly surrender to God in all things. Any trials that come to us must be accepted joyfully as we place our hope in our weaknesses in God. . . . (2 Cor. 12:9-10). (*In Jesus We Trust*, Maloney; p. 134.)

We are chosen, blessed, and broken so as to be given. . . . For me, personally, this means that it is only as people who are given that we can fully understand our being chosen, blessed, and broken. In the giving it becomes clear that we are chosen, blessed, and broken not simply for our own sakes, but so that all we live finds its final significance in its being lived for others. (*Life of the Beloved*, Henri J. M. Nouwen; p. 84.)

Reflection Time

Making Our Requests Known
Prayer for Our World, Its People and Leaders
Prayer for the Church and Its Leaders
Prayer for Those in Our Circle of Responsibility
Prayer for Ourselves

Offering of Self to God
Because of this many of his disciples turned back and no longer went about with him. So Jesus asked the twelve, "Do you also wish to go

away?" Simon Peter answered him, "Lord, to whom can we go? You have the words of eternal life. We have come to believe and know that you are the Holy One of God." (John 6:66-69)

Blessing
Surely God is my salvation;
    I will trust and will not be afraid,
for the Lord God is my strength and my might;
    he has become my salvation. (Isaiah 12:2)

Week 18

LIFE TRANSFORMED

Becoming Aware of God's Presence

Tender Shepherd, who promised to be with us always, we welcome you now into our midst and invite you to stay with us all the day long.

Inviting God's Intervention

Come tender Shepherd and be our guide, strength, and companion in every experience of life today and always.

Listening for God's Voice

Sunday	*A.* Exodus 17:1-7; Psalm 95; Romans 5:1-11; John 4:5-42
	B. Exodus 20:1-17; Psalm 19; 1 Corinthians 1:18-25; John 2:13-22
	C. Isaiah 55:1-9; Psalm 63:1-8; 1 Corinthians 10:1-13; Luke 13:1-9
Monday	Romans 12:1-8
Tuesday	Romans 12:14-21
Wednesday	Romans 13:8-14
Thursday	Matthew 5:13-16
Friday	Philippians 1:3-11
Saturday	John 17:1-11

Essay

Living a transformed life does not happen by gritting our teeth and trying harder. It happens as we offer ourselves ever more fully to the One who knows us completely and loves us beyond our ability to comprehend. Of course, we are called to live a disciplined and faithful life, but not on our own. It is God who leads us, strengthens us, and sustains us in a life of faithfulness. And it is God who does the transforming work as we open ourselves more and more to the Spirit's presence, guidance, and grace. Paul's confession in 2 Corinthians 3:18 says it well: "And all of us, with unveiled faces, seeing the glory of the Lord as though reflected in a mirror, are being transformed into the same image from one degree of glory to another; for this comes from the Lord, the Spirit." When we spend our days and nights in God's presence, we too will reflect that divine image more and more. This is God's transforming work in progress in ordinary lives and ordinary times. May it always be the story of our lives.

Quotations

Every Christian practice requires prayer, as Christians doing things together attune themselves to take part, with trust, in the risky activities of God. In prayer, we open ourselves to respond to God's presence and notice the light of God as it shines on the world, exposing fault yet also promising hope. We pay attention in a special way, focusing our yearning to be partners in God's reconciling love. We ask for God's help in saying yes to that which is life-giving in the deepest sense and in saying the specific no that will loosen whatever chains bind us and others to destruction. We thank God for life and love, and we beg God for mercy and strength, for ourselves and all creation. (*Practicing Our Faith*, Bass; p. 202.)

The prayer practice known as THE EXAMEN helps us to see the will of God in action. . . . The key to understanding the examen as a practice of discernment is to see how looking backward to identify the movement of God can lead to being guided by God in the future. . . . The examen asks us to look back over a period of time or review an event, looking for glimmers, moments, and actions that appear to be either "of God" or not "of God." The former are the life-giving things that bring the fruits of the Spirit, while the latter are those things that are death-dealing and bring fruits of a spirit that is not God. . . . The prayerful *examen*-ation of the past helps us in our discernment of the future because we begin to see the trajectory of God's action in our place and our time. (*Leading a Life With God*, Wolpert; pp. 68–69.)

The Christ who calls us from the depths of our being, who commissions us to witness to what we know in our hearts, is the one who brings life abundant, not only to us but through us, the church and its members. Each of us chooses to be part of this world's problems or its solutions, a connection or disconnection from God's love, a spark fed by the fire of God's Spirit or one that flies from the fire and dies alone. Jesus was a realist. "In the world you face persecution," he stated, "but take courage; I have conquered the world" (John 16:33). (*Faith, the Yes of the Heart*, Brame; p. 92.)

Along [sic] time ago, I heard Jean Houston tell a story about herself as a youth, going to hear a presentation by Helen Keller who was blind and deaf. Houston said that after Helen Keller finished speaking she knew that she had to talk with her. She got up and presented her face to Helen Keller. Jean Houston described the experience this way: "She read my whole face and I blurted out: 'Miss Keller, why are you so happy?' and she laughed and laughed, saying: 'My child, it is because I live each day as if it were my last and life, with all its moments, is so full of glory.' " (*The Cup of Our Life*, Joyce Rupp; p. 145.)

Reflection Time

Making Our Requests Known
Prayer for Our World, Its People and Leaders
Prayer for the Church and Its Leaders
Prayer for Those in Our Circle of Responsibility
Prayer for Ourselves

Offering of Self to God

In trust and love we now offer all that we are and have to you and ask you to accept, bless, and use the gift we bring in ways that are pleasing to you; for we know that will be good and right for us.

Blessing

Bless and make fruitful the life we offer, this day and always, for we are yours.

Week 19
JESUS DOES THE UNEXPECTED

Becoming Aware of God's Presence

O LORD, I have heard of your renown,
   and I stand in awe, O LORD, of your work.
In our own time revive it;
   in our own time make it known;
   in wrath may you remember mercy. (Habakkuk 3:2)

Inviting God's Intervention

GOD, the Lord, is my strength;
   he makes my feet like the feet of a deer,
   and makes me tread upon the heights. (Habakkuk 3:19)

Listening for God's Voice

Sunday	*A.* 1 Samuel 16:1-13; Psalm 23; Ephesians 5:8-14; John 9:1-41
	B. Numbers 21:4-9; Psalm 107:1-3, 17-22; Ephesians 2:1-10; John 3:14-21
	C. Joshua 5:9-12; Psalm 32; 2 Corinthians 5:16-21; Luke 15:1-3, 11b-32
Monday	Luke 17:1-19
Tuesday	Jeremiah 1:4-10
Wednesday	Mark 12:13-17
Thursday	Matthew 20:1-16
Friday	Mark 2:13-17
Saturday	Luke 22:24-37

Essay

Jesus often catches us off guard and we are surprised by what he says and does. Just when we think we know Jesus really well, he surprises us and leaves us trying to catch our breath and catch up to where he is and where he is trying to lead us. These days leading up to his crucifixion and resurrection are no exception. Eugene H. Peterson, in the introduction to his book *Tell It Slant*, says, "As we listen in on Jesus as he talks and then participate with Jesus as he prays, I hope that together we, writer and readers, will develop a discerning aversion to all forms of depersonalizing godtalk that acquire a taste for and skills in the always personal language God uses, even in our conversations and small talk, maybe especially in our small talk, to make and save and bless us one and all" (p. 5). The chapters that follow make it clear that it was not just the language of Jesus that was clear and straightforward, but his actions as well. Jesus consistently did the unexpected and he told stories about everyday events in unexpected ways to carry the truth of his out-of-the-ordinary message and life.

Quotations

Just as we're checking off boxes down a long, dreary list of the bad we've not—or mostly not—done, we hear Jesus explaining from across the room, on the other side of the punch bowl, *You've heard it was said . . . long ago, 'You shall not murder,'. . . But I tell you that anyone who is angry with a brother or sister will be subject to judgment. . . .* And Jesus goes on from there, leaving no cobwebbed corner of our insides unseen: Lust. Selfishness. Deceit. Revenge. Greed. Pettiness. Pride. . . . Holiness, real holiness, the kind Jesus presents, is not about chains or checklists but hunger. And longing. Finding ourselves desperate for meaning, for purpose, for something bigger and richer and beyond the tawdry this-world that we let define us. Wishing to wipe down the slates of our pasts, clean up our acts, start over again. To live this time for something higher and wider and deeper. More wild. More dangerous. . . . More holy. (*Why Jesus Makes Me Nervous*, Jordan-Lake; pp. 45–46.)

I have long been taken by the origin of the name "Christian." In Acts 11 there was a community of people who so lived out the Christ-life that they were called "Christians," which means "little Christs." There is no sense that it was ever a term of derision or ridicule—just an observation. Here were people living a life that reflected the person of Jesus. What should the perceptions of Christians be in thirty years? That there is something supernatural about our lives, that there is something about us that cannot be explained in anything other than a miraculous way. . . . I think of the scandal of grace in the midst of community, the selflessness of compassion in the face of disdain, the aroma of holiness in the teeth of debauchery, the firmness of orthodoxy while immersed in the illusion of various matrices. But most of all, I suppose, I think of the scandal of grace—freely received into our lives and then freely distributed to others. Jesus himself said this should be the mark of the Christian, and the single dynamic that would arrest the world's attention. (Jim White quoted in *Unchristian*, David Kinnaman and Gabe Lyons; p. 237.)

This birth of Jesus, this death of Jesus, this resurrection of Jesus—is something we cannot do for ourselves, cannot take credit for, cannot take over and run with, cannot reproduce in any way. It is done for us. We can only hear and believe and enter this God-for-us-reality that is so generously given as both the context and the content of our lives. (*Christ Plays in Ten Thousand Places*, Peterson; p. 231.)

We need to become ever more sensitive to the call to prayer, be it external or inward. Our divine adoption means that we are in a continuous relationship with God at the level of being. For the most part we are unaware of this. So we need to listen closely, especially if we find it difficult to distinguish God's footsteps among the welter of interior noises. *The Cloud of Unknowing* calls the interior invitations to prayer "stirrings." From time to time God's presence is felt within us and we are invited to respond. Such incidents occur unpredictably and without preparation—in a pause between tasks, as a background to other activities or in a time of leisure. They may burst into consciousness, making it difficult to continue whatever we were doing. They may even arouse us from sleep. In an obscure and undefined way we become aware that our whole self is being drawn toward God in a manner fundamentally independent of our conscious willing. (*Toward God*, Casey; p. 49.)

Reflection Time

Making Our Requests Known
Prayer for Our World, Its People and Leaders
Prayer for the Church and Its Leaders
Prayer for Those in Our Circle of Responsibility
Prayer for Ourselves

Offering of Self to God
Here am I, your loving creature, offering all that I am and hope to become to you, my loving Creator. Accept the gift I bring and make it fruitful as you keep me faithful, for I am yours.

Blessing
May the God of peace and love dwell within us, accompany us, guide us, and keep us throughout the day and always. Amen.

Week 20

HOPE: PROMISE AND FULFILLMENT

Becoming Aware of God's Presence

Let your work be manifest to your servants,
    and your glorious power to their children. (Psalm 90:16)

Inviting God's Intervention

Satisfy us in the morning with your steadfast love,
    so that we may rejoice and be glad all our days. (Psalm 90:14)

Listening for God's Voice

Sunday	**A.** Ezekiel 37:1-14; Psalm 130; Romans 8:6-11; John 11:1-45
	B. Jeremiah 31:31-34; Psalm 51:1-12; Hebrews 5:5-10; John 12:20-33
	C. Isaiah 43:16-21; Psalm 126; Philippians 3:4b-14; John 12:1-8
Monday	Ephesians 1:15-23
Tuesday	Acts 23:1-12
Wednesday	1 Peter 1:3-9
Thursday	1 Peter 1:13-21
Friday	1 Peter 1:22-25
Saturday	Ephesians 2:11-22

Essay

My hopes are often so timid and tame that I hardly notice when they don't come to pass. So it did rain when I was going to mow the lawn. Small matter. Not at all like the hope about which our Scriptures speak this week. Here is hope at the very center of life. It is hope that is the promise of earthshaking and life-changing magnitude. You and I are children of God who are promised our full inheritance as God's beloved. Why should we fear? The living God has promised to be our companion in every experience of life, in this world and the next. No one can separate us from God or from our inheritance as a child of God. It is ours and by God's grace we may claim it now. Paul put it this way, "I pray that the God of our Lord Jesus Christ, the Father of glory, may give you a spirit of wisdom and revelation as you come to know him, so that, with the eyes of your heart enlightened, you may know what is the hope to which he has called you, what are the riches of his glorious inheritance among the saints . . ." (Ephesians 1:17-18).

Hope for wild, wonderful, and too-good-to-be-true results like actual signs of God's kingdom sprouting up all over the world, in your community, and even in your life. And then let your life and your prayer reflect that hope this day and always. Your kingdom come on *earth* as it is in *heaven*. May it be so today!

Quotations

It has been said that Charles Wesley's hymns always begin on earth and end in heaven. So it is with John Wesley's theology. He was firmly convinced of the coming day of Christ, which is not yet, but toward which humankind, with the whole creation, is moving. For Wesley, it was necessary to stress God's ultimate victory; but it was also important to affirm the penultimate reality of God's presence, now experienced as life that is drawn to God in increasingly focused love. John Wesley had a doctrine of final things, an eschatology, in which God's kingdom is being presently realized even as it points toward a consummating future. The Christian lives with the lively hope that God, who has begun a good thing, will fulfill it in the day of Jesus Christ. (*Practical Divinity*, Vol. 1, Thomas A. Langford; pp. 36–37.)

It is impossible to exaggerate the historical significance and the endless personal ramifications of salvation. It always exceeds our powers of understanding and imagining. We will never get our minds around it. We see well enough what is going on: God is at work in history; he heals and helps; he forgives and blesses; he takes creation in ruins because of human willfulness and patiently begins to make a new creation of it; he takes a world corrupted by evil and begins the long slow work of transforming it into a holy place. But we see all this in bits and pieces, moments and fragments. It is understandable that we often reduce salvation to a handful of . . . fragments. But we must not. We are dealing with God's work in history on a scale of comprehensiveness that ever eludes us. St. Paul, wrapping up his excursus on God's salvation work in history in his Letter to the Romans, is appropriately in awe of what we will never grasp: "O the depth of the riches and wisdom and knowledge of God! How unsearchable are his judgments and how inscrutable his ways!" (Rom. 11:33). (*Christ Plays in Ten Thousand Places*, Peterson; pp. 169–170.)

"Anyone who follows me shall not walk in darkness," says the Lord. These are the words of Christ, and by them we are reminded that we must imitate his life and his ways if we are to be truly enlightened and set free from the darkness of our own hearts. Let it be the most important thing we do, then, to reflect on the life of Jesus Christ. Christ's teaching surpasses all the teachings of the saints, and the person who has his spirit will find hidden nourishment in his words. (*The Imitation of Christ*, Thomas À Kempis; p. 30.)

"We are children of a double order and ought to expect as both natural and spiritual creatures, another life to live here and now." That other life is our inheritance. Sadly, says Underhill, there are those of us who know we have been offered such a legacy, but whose lives are too full of our other riches to find room for this special gift. We do not realize that we will receive as much of the kingdom of heaven as suits our souls. Furthermore, it is an inheritance given not hereafter, but now, and what we receive and live in now will become our home for eternity. . . . It is the presence of God which is our true home, the country of the soul. It is there that we belong. It is that which we claim. (From Grace Adolphsen Brame's Introduction to *The Ways of the Spirit*, Evelyn Underhill; p. 35.)

Reflection Time

Making Our Requests Known
Prayer for Our World, Its People and Leaders
Prayer for the Church and Its Leaders
Prayer for Those in Our Circle of Responsibility
Prayer for Ourselves

Offering of Self to God
It is good to give thanks to the LORD,
    to sing praises to your name, O Most High;
to declare your steadfast love in the morning,
    and your faithfulness by night, . . .
For you, O LORD, have made me glad by your work;
    at the works of your hands I sing for joy. (Psalm 92:1-2, 4)

Blessing
Let the favor of the Lord our God be upon us,
    and prosper for us the work of our hands—
    O prosper the work of our hands! (Psalm 90:17)

Week 21
TRUTH ON TRIAL

Palm / Passion Sunday

Becoming Aware of God's Presence

In you, O LORD, I take refuge;
   let me never be put to shame.
In your righteousness deliver me and rescue me;
   incline your ear to me and save me.
Be to me a rock of refuge,
   a strong fortress, to save me,
   for you are my rock and my fortress. (Psalm 71:1-3)

Inviting God's Intervention

Rescue me, O my God, from the hand of the wicked,
   from the grasp of the unjust and cruel.
For you, O Lord, are my hope,
   my trust, O LORD, from my youth. (Psalm 71:4-5)

Listening for God's Voice

Sunday	*A.* Isaiah 50:4-9a; Psalm 31:9-16; Philippians 2:5-11; Matthew 27:11-54
	B. Isaiah 50:4-9a; Psalm 31:9-16; Philippians 2:5-11; Mark 15:1-39, (40-47)
	C. Isaiah 50:4-9a; Psalm 31:9-16; Philippians 2:5-11; Luke 23:1-49
Monday	Psalm 71:12-18
Tuesday	John 13:21-30
Wednesday	Hebrews 12:1-3
Thursday	1 Corinthians 1:18-25
Friday	1 Peter 4:1-11
Saturday	1 Peter 4:12-19

Essay

Jesus got into a lot of trouble in his brief ministry and it was always for all the right reasons. His message was radical and dangerous to the ears of religious and political leaders. However, this same message was wonderful, redeeming truth to the average, the poor, and the oppressed persons of his time. This week's Scripture readings give us a glimpse of his final days, including his trial and crucifixion. Jesus said, "Whoever has seen me has seen the Father" (John 14:9). And the writer of Colossians says, "He is the image of the invisible God" (1:15). It is clear from the Scripture record that the reality of truth, righteousness, and goodness were on trial with Jesus. Jesus begins his week as the prince of peace and ends it as an executed criminal. It may seem as though truth, goodness, righteousness, and God have lost it all in this one week of confrontation. Fortunately, it is not the end of the story. That comes next week. In the meantime, we ask ourselves, "How are we doing in telling the truth about goodness, righteousness, Jesus, and God?"

Quotations

I do see the future Christian faith being something that is good, true, and credible in our culture. I can dream of a day when the followers of Jesus are known not for these current tragic perceptions, but for trying to live like Jesus. We will fumble, stumble, and hit some rough patches along the way, but we must not give up. I look forward to the day when Christian hangouts won't just be Sunday morning church services or praise-band practices, but instead Tuesday night potlucks at the local homeless shelter. One day the world will ask, "Where are all those Christian freaks at?" I pray our answer will be, "We're over here helping in the ravaged slums of Africa and happily drilling wells in Haitian villages. And, guys, we're going to be here for a while." . . . Christians will be the first to sound the cry of injustice and rally the nations that we all must do more. We will have officially burned the Christian "bandwagon" and become a people who from the beginning rallied for the oppressed, forgotten, and overlooked. And when we cry out against wrongs and evils in this world, people will listen and know what we say is true because our words will sound a lot like those of our Savior. (Mike Foster quoted in *Unchristian*, Kinnaman and Lyons; pp. 242–243.)

When I think about the spiritual life, I think of a life with God that is healthy and vibrant. The root and foundation of this life is *relationship*. This relationship may have many struggles, crooked paths, and hidden corners but at the core there is a bond that is deep and strong. This relationship feeds and nourishes my inner self and gives a vitality and vibrancy to all of my life. Each one of us is a temple of the Holy One. Each of us carries a spiritual power in us that can cause even the tiniest of faith-seeds to grow. It is vital that we protect and nurture this relationship so that it thrives. The cup of our spiritual life must be cared for and replenished as it pours its contents away in loving service. Like the cup with its boundaries, we, too, need parameters so that our life does not seep away into endless busy-ness and unguarded, unfocused activity. (*The Cup of Our Life*, Rupp; p. 22.)

The work of following Christ is like working with a psychotherapist who has a clear insight into what is wrong with us. With incredible accuracy, God puts his finger on exactly the spot that needs attention at this precise time in our spiritual growth. If we are hanging on to one last shred of possessiveness, he comes along and says, often through some person or event, "Won't you give this to me?" (*Invitation to Love*, Thomas Keating; p. 18.)

Most of us have a strong desire to deepen and strengthen our sense of living with God in the daily activities of life. In our better moments we want a more intimate relationship with God. We really do want to experience God's companionship in all of life because we know that life is incomplete without this central experience of God. We want to claim and to enjoy our full inheritance as children of God. . . . John Wesley saw and experienced what we see and experience. It is impossible to live as a Christian if we are unattached to

God. Our spiritual and even our physical lives become a shambles without the constant companionship with God that prayer alone can make possible. (*A Wesleyan Spiritual Reader*, Job; p. 15.)

Jesus chose the way of peace in a violent world. He taught his disciples to do the same. Just for a moment Peter forgot, and because of that, one of the arresting party lost an ear. But still Jesus rebuked Peter and courageously continued his journey as the Prince of Peace on the way to his own death. (*A Guide to Prayer for All Who Seek God*, Norman Shawchuck and Rueben P. Job; p. 164.)

Reflection Time

Making Our Requests Known
Prayer for Our World, Its People and Leaders
Prayer for the Church and Its Leaders
Prayer for Those in Our Circle of Responsibility
Prayer for Ourselves

Offering of Self to God
Humble yourselves therefore under the mighty hand of God, so that he may exalt you in due time. Cast all your anxiety on him, because he cares for you. Discipline yourselves, keep alert. (1 Peter 5:6-8a)

Blessing
May grace and peace rest upon us to guide, strengthen, and keep us as we seek to follow the way of Christ. May it be so today and always.

Week 22
JESUS GOES ON AHEAD

Easter Sunday

Becoming Aware of God's Presence
While they were talking and discussing, Jesus himself came near and went with them . . . (Luke 24:15)

Inviting God's Intervention
But they urged him strongly, saying, "Stay with us, because it is almost evening and the day is now nearly over." So he went in to stay with them. (Luke 24:29)

Listening for God's Voice

Sunday	*A.* Jeremiah 31:1-6; Psalm 118:1-2, 14-24; Colossians 3:1-4; John 20:1-18
	B. Isaiah 25:6-9; Psalm 118:1-2, 14-24; 1 Corinthians 15:1-11; Mark 16:1-8
	C. Acts 10:34-43; Psalm 118:1-2, 14-24; 1 Corinthians 15:19-26; Luke 24:1-12
Monday	Matthew 28:1-10
Tuesday	John 14:1-14
Wednesday	Acts 3:1-16
Thursday	Isaiah 25:1-9
Friday	Acts 4:1-12
Saturday	Acts 4:13-31

Essay
It was a great comfort for me to have my father on ahead with his plow and five horses creating an arrow-straight, half-mile-long furrow. I followed along with my smaller plow and three horses confident that if I simply kept one wheel of the plow in the furrow I would leave that

arrow-straight furrow behind me as well. It was a comfort to have him on ahead because he knew where the rocky and muddy areas were and when to lift the plow to preserve the grassed-over waterways.

There was one other reason I wanted to stay close to him. I couldn't have explained it then. But now, in my eight decades of life, I know it was the desire for his company that kept me close. Even then, young boys had their own questions of self-worth, their own feelings of loneliness, and their own anxiety about tomorrow. But in the company of my father, the one whose love had never failed or forsaken me, all was well. Neither cold nor rain could drive me away. For even then I knew all was well in the company of the one who seemed to know how to do everything and who loved me so deeply. Jesus spoke to the women visiting the tomb, "Do not be afraid; go and tell my brothers to go to Galilee; there they will see me" (Matthew 28:10). Who are you following into the future?

Quotations

Those who have apprenticed themselves to Jesus learn an undying life with a future as good and as large as God himself. The experiences we have of this life as his co-conspirators now fill us with anticipation of a future so full of beauty and goodness we can hardly imagine. "When Christ, who is our life, shall appear," Paul says, "then you too will be revealed with him as glorious" (Col. 3:4). And, "How great a love the Father has lavished upon us," John exclaims, "that we should be described as children of God! But it has not yet been shown what we shall be. We only know that when he appears we shall be as he is" (1 John 3: 1-2). Reverting to Paul, "He will transform our lowly body to be like his glory body, using the power he has over everything" (Phil. 3:[21]). (*The Divine Conspiracy*, Willard; pp. 375–376.)

Prayer is our means of taking a sighting, of re-orienting ourselves—by re-establishing contact with our goal. In the presence of God many components of our life fall into perspective and our journey begins to make more sense. We look toward God, conscious that seeking what is unseen corresponds to a very deep stratum of our being. It is not just a bright idea or a fad; it grows from the soil of the heart. Prayer is inseparable from living. The worst thing we can think about prayer is that it is a trivial exercise—saying a few words or channeling one's thoughts in a particular direction. Authentic prayer is not that. It is usually difficult. This is not because it takes great expertise or is reserved to an elite, but because it takes a lot of courage. To pray well I must first find out where I am. Self-knowledge is never procured cheaply. To pray well I need to face up to realities about myself, that I would prefer to ignore: my anxieties, fears, private griefs, failures, lovelessness, my utter lack of resources. To accept the truth about what I am, as also the truth about other human beings, demands courage. If I do not pray well, it is usually because I lack that kind of courage. (*Toward God*, Casey; p. 5.)

All four Gospel writers conclude their Jesus story with his resurrection. But John does something additional which calls for special attention as we attend to the significance of the *community* of the resurrection. The text that holds this in focus is this: "[Jesus] breathed on them [his assembled disciples] and said to them, 'Receive the Holy Spirit' (John 20:22)." A few days before the resurrection, on the evening before his crucifixion, Jesus had an extended conversation with his disciples that prepared them for his death and resurrection. Throughout that conversation he promised them over and over again, with variations, that when he was gone physically he would be present with them in the Spirit (John 14:15-17, 25-26; 15:26; 16:7-11, 13-14). On the day of resurrection he made good on that promise: "Receive the Holy Spirit." He replaced himself with himself. Resurrection is the work of the Holy Spirit in Jesus, raising him from the dead and presenting him before the disciples; resurrection is also the work of the Holy Spirit in those of us who believe in and follow Jesus. (*Christ Plays in Ten Thousand Places*, Peterson; p. 232.)

This kind of blessing prayer is called a benediction. It comes at the end of something, to send people on their way. All I am saying is that anyone can do this. Anyone can ask and anyone can bless, whether anyone has authorized you to do it or not. All I am saying is that the world needs you to do this, because there is a real shortage of people willing to kneel wherever they are and recognize the holiness holding its sometimes bony, often tender, always life-giving hand above their heads. That we are able to bless one another at all is evidence that we have been blessed, whether we can remember when or not. That we are willing to bless one another is miracle enough to stagger the very stars. (*An Altar in the World*, Barbara Brown Taylor; pp. 208–209.)

Reflection Time

Making Our Requests Known
Prayer for Our World, Its People and Leaders
Prayer for the Church and Its Leaders
Prayer for Those in Our Circle of Responsibility
Prayer for Ourselves

Offering of Self to God
He came to Simon Peter, who said to him, "Lord, are you going to wash my feet?" Jesus answered, "You do not know now what I am doing, but later you will understand." Peter said to him, "You will never wash my feet." Jesus answered, "Unless I wash you, you have no share with me." Simon Peter said to him, "Lord, not my feet only but also my hands and my head!" (John 13:6-9)

Blessing
Jesus said to them again, "Peace be with you. As the Father has sent me, so I send you." When he had said this, he breathed on them and said to them, "Receive the Holy Spirit." (John 20:21-22)

Week 23
YOU CAN TRUST ME

Becoming Aware of God's Presence

My heart is steadfast, O God, my heart is steadfast;
   I will sing and make melody.
   Awake, my soul! . . .
For your steadfast love is higher than the heavens,
   and your faithfulness reaches to the clouds. (Psalm 108:1, 4)

Inviting God's Intervention

Give justice to the weak and the orphan;
   maintain the right of the lowly and the destitute.
Rescue the weak and the needy;
   deliver them from the hand of the wicked. (Psalm 82:3-4)

Listening for God's Voice

Sunday	*A.* Acts 2:14a, 22-32; Psalm 16; 1 Peter 1:3-9; John 20:19-31
	B. Acts 4:32-35; Psalm 133; 1 John 1:1–2:2; John 20:19-31
	C. Acts 5:27-32; Psalm 118:14-29; Revelation 1:4-8; John 20:19-31
Monday	Hebrews 2:1-13
Tuesday	John 4:39-45
Wednesday	Psalm 28:6-9
Thursday	1 John 5:1-5
Friday	1 Peter 1:3-9
Saturday	John 16:16-24

Essay

Thomas wanted to see for himself. Paul when giving witness to the Church at Corinth used his own experience of the living Christ as proof of the reality of the Resurrection. We can understand the desire for that once-and-for-all physical proof that Jesus is alive and in our midst. When our dreams are cruelly crushed, as were those that Thomas had, we too begin to wonder, can we really trust Jesus and his promise to never forsake us? Or, are we on our own? Two thousand years of history tell us, "Yes, we can trust him," and, "No, we are never alone." God has granted the gift of long life to me and while I have never put my hands in the wounds of Jesus, I am more confident than ever that God is with me and that the testimony of the early church is trustworthy. "I am convinced that neither death, nor life, nor angels, nor rulers, nor things present, nor things to come, nor powers, nor height, nor depth, nor anything else in all creation, will be able to separate us from the love of God in Christ Jesus our Lord" (Romans 8:38-39). This is enough for me. How about you?

Quotations

In his sonnet "The Resurrection," John Donne wrote, "He was all gold when he lay down, but rose / All tincture." Donne was referring to alchemy, whose ultimate object was not just to turn baser metals into gold, but to discover a tincture that would turn any metal it touched into gold. The risen Christ had become this tincture, turning the lives he touched into "gold." Thenceforth, his people would be Jesus's body, doing what he would do if he still had physical hands and feet. (*The Soul of Christianity*, Smith; pp. 74–75.)

Answers do come to prayers, both clear and unclear answers. What starts as an anxious query to God—"Are you there? Do you hear me?"—or a defiant demand—"Prove it to me! Show me a sign!"—turns into fear in the presence of the holy. What begins as worry that our prayers are not answered, ends, if we keep praying, in awe that answers really do come. When that happens, we grow cautious about what we pray for. (*Primary Speech*, Ulanov; p. 99.)

The gist of the post-resurrectional message of Jesus to his disciples has been summed up in the words, "Peace! I am alive. There is work for you to do." This message points not only to the ground of intercessory prayer but to the re-enlistment the full resources of the one who prays into the labor force of the kingdom of God. Indeed there is work for you to do and real prayer seldom concludes without some intimation of a work assignment. For if prayer in one sense is a disengagement—a stepping aside from life in order to look at it in the deepest perspective, to see it under the gaze of God—it does not stop there. (*Dimensions of Prayer*, Steere; p. 95.)

The story does not end there. Early in the morning two days later Mary Magdalene and the other women disciples went to the tomb with oils for a last anointing of Jesus' body. Instead of a corpse they encountered the living Christ and bore witness of this to the other disciples. As events raced on the conviction of faith rose up: The raising of the dead which was supposed to happen on the last day with the coming of the reign of God has already begun to happen. By the loving power of God Jesus is transformed into glory, he is raised up. Such existence is beyond our imagination, for it is life in another dimension beyond the limits of time and space; it is life in the dimension of God. It is better symbolized in the Easter Vigil liturgy, with its dramatic scenes of light out of darkness, proclamation of the creation story, sprinkling the water of new life, and sharing the eucharistic bread. Rather than coming to nothing in death, Jesus died into God. He is risen, whole and entire, as the embodied person he was in this life—his wounds are a sign of that. (*Consider Jesus*, Johnson; pp. 59–60.)

Reflection Time

Making Our Requests Known
Prayer for Our World, Its People and Leaders
Prayer for the Church and Its Leaders
Prayer for Those in Our Circle of Responsibility
Prayer for Ourselves

Offering of Self to God

But I trusted in your steadfast love;
  my heart shall rejoice in your salvation.
I will sing to the LORD,
  because he has dealt bountifully with me. (Psalm 13:5-6)

Blessing

The LORD bless you and keep you;
the LORD make his face to shine
  upon you, and be gracious to you;
the LORD lift up his countenance upon you,
  and give you peace. (Numbers 6:24-26)

Week 24
WHEN FAITH OVERCOMES FEAR

Becoming Aware of God's Presence

When I think of your ways,
    I turn my feet to your decrees;
I hurry and do not delay
    to keep your commandments. (Psalm 119:59-60)

Inviting God's Intervention

Your hands have made and fashioned me;
    give me understanding that I may learn your commandments.
(Psalm 119:73)

Listening for God's Voice

Sunday	*A.* Acts 2:14a, 36-41; Psalm 116:1-4, 12-19; 1 Peter 1:17-23; Luke 24:13-35
	B. Acts 3:12-19; Psalm 4; 1 John 3:1-7; Luke 24:36b-48
	C. Acts 9:1-6, (7-20); Psalm 30; Revelation 5:11-14; John 21:1-19
Monday	Philippians 1:12-18
Tuesday	Matthew 10:24-31
Wednesday	Luke 12:32-34
Thursday	1 Thessalonians 1
Friday	1 Peter 3:8-22
Saturday	Colossians 3:1-11

Essay

With dreams dashed and hopes riddled by fear the followers of Jesus sought to make sense of the past and chart a new course for the future. The sights and sounds of the public execution of their leader were impossible to forget, and the danger did not go away. As their numbers grew so did the dangers that stalked them day and night. It is not surprising that sometimes fear kept them behind closed doors. What is surprising is that their faith conquered their fear and transformed them into confident, bold, and effective witnesses to the life, death, resurrection, and message of Jesus. Their words and their lives were in harmony with the gospel, and this new movement quickly attracted large numbers of followers.

There are still places today where the danger of persecution stalks the followers of Christ and fear is an ever-present reality. For most of us, our fears are of a different nature, but are no less real. It was faith in the presence of Jesus in their midst and on their journey that overcame fear in those early disciples. It is still the perfect response to fear today. Let's remind each other and ourselves every day this week that Jesus is in our midst and walks with each of us in our journey of life. Thanks be to God!

Quotations
The first Christians who spread the Good News throughout the Mediterranean world did not feel that they were alone. They were not even alone together, for they believed that Jesus was in their midst as a concrete, energizing power. They remembered that he had said, "Where two or three are gathered in my name, I am there among them.["] So, while their contemporaries were nicknaming the Christians (literally "the Messiah-folk," because they believed Jesus to be the redeemer the prophets had foretold), they began to call themselves an *ekklesia*. In the Greek of their day this meant no more than a self-governing assembly, but for the Christians the assembly was not a self-help society, a merely human association in which people of goodwill banded together to encourage one another in good works and lift themselves by their collective bootstraps. Human members constituted the Christian *ekklesia*, but it was powered by Christ's— read God's—presence within it. The English word for this would be "church." (*The Soul of Christianity*, Smith; pp. 84–85.)

Prayer will carry us far into the paschal mystery, though there will be times when we believe ourselves utterly alienated from any spiritual process. Everything in us that is hostile to God must be uncovered, and its bitterness tasted, before we can eliminate it. We will begin to wonder whether anything will survive such radical purgation. All that remains, in fact, will be what God has created and restored. Of our own unaided work and achievements there will be nothing. Our glory is to be transparent. If the face of God shines through us, we will be perfect in both beauty and happiness. Efforts to leave our mark result only in obscuring that radiance. (*Toward God*, Casey; p. 158.)

In the resurrection, the Spirit of God fills Jesus with new life and, present in the community in a new way, he becomes the cornerstone of the coming reign of God. His Spirit is poured out on all who believe, women equally with men. The early Christians adopted the initiation rite of baptism. Unlike the gender-specific Jewish ritual of circumcision, open only to males, baptism is inclusive since it is administered the same way to persons of both genders. Indicative of this, Paul's letter to the Galatians contains an early Christian baptismal hymn. As the newly baptized come up out of the water, all in white, wet robes, they sing, "Now there is no more Jew or Greek, slave or free, male or female, but all are one in Christ Jesus" (3:28). All divisions based on race, or class, or even gender are transcended in the oneness of the body of Christ. The power of the risen Christ becomes effective to the extent that this vision becomes reality in the community. (*Consider Jesus*, Johnson; p. 111.)

In the Emmaus Resurrection story, we have a powerful and moving picture of Jesus coming alongside two of his disciples on the road (and notice that they are not of the inner circle of the apostles). He walks with them; he is concerned about their sadness, and he continues to be their teacher as he was in life. He responds to their desire for his continued company—"stay with us"—and joins them for a meal. In the familiar gesture of taking, blessing and breaking bread, at last their eyes are opened, and they recognize their companion on the road. Then they can recognize also that he had kindled their hearts in his teaching on the Scriptures, in the way he helped them to see afresh the familiar stories of patriarchs and prophets and the history of their people. I find this a marvelous parable for the Christian life. While most of us will have times set aside for prayer, for coming together in worship and fellowship, perhaps for solitude or for study, most of it happens "on the road." . . . As he travels with us, he makes himself known in word and sacrament—in the opening of the Scriptures, and the breaking of the bread. (*The Road to Emmaus*, Helen Julian, C. S. F.; pp. 177–178.)

Reflection Time

Making Our Requests Known
Prayer for Our World, Its People and Leaders
Prayer for the Church and Its Leaders
Prayer for Those in Our Circle of Responsibility
Prayer for Ourselves

Offering of Self to God
I will never forget your precepts,
> for by them you have given me life.
I am yours; save me,
> for I have sought your precepts. (Psalm 119:93-94)

Blessing
Turn to me and be gracious to me,
> as is your custom toward those who love your name.
Keep my steps steady according to your promise,
> and never let iniquity have dominion over me. (Psalm 119:132-133)

Week 25
THE GOOD SHEPHERD

Becoming Aware of God's Presence
The LORD is my shepherd, I shall not want. (Psalm 23:1)

Inviting God's Intervention
Make me to know your ways, O LORD;
    teach me your paths.
Lead me in your truth, and teach me,
    for you are the God of my salvation;
    for you I wait all day long. (Psalm 25:4-5)

Listening for God's Voice

Sunday	*A.* Acts 2:42-47; Psalm 23; 1 Peter 2:19-25; John 10:1-10
	B. Acts 4:5-12; Psalm 23; 1 John 3:16-24; John 10:11-18
	C. Acts 9:36-43; Psalm 23; Revelation 7:9-17; John 10:22-30
Monday	Isaiah 40:6-11
Tuesday	Ezekiel 34:11-16
Wednesday	Isaiah 25:1-9
Thursday	Ezekiel 34:25-31
Friday	Matthew 9:35-38
Saturday	Luke 13:22-30

Essay
The late winter storm came up quickly with high winds that forced the heavy snow into large drifts and made movement of our small flock of sheep almost impossible. At the first sign of the storm my father took his three sons to gather up the sheep and put them into a dry

barn with straw for bedding and hay we carried in for them to eat. We had a large number of cattle on our farm but only a few sheep to complete a 4-H project for my two older brothers and me. The goal was to learn all about raising sheep so that they could be a profitable part of our diversified farm. We had already learned that they were gentle and lovable animals and that they had a tendency to nibble their way into trouble. Now we learned another of their weaknesses in the midst of a late winter North Dakota snowstorm.

Jesus describes himself as "the good shepherd" who knows and understands the ways of every sheep and will lay down his life for their well-being. For me it is a strong image of God's knowledge of each of us and of God's love and care for each of us. The Gospel readings from John and the Twenty-third Psalm continue to be a great source of comfort, security, and hope for me as I learn to trust and follow the Good Shepherd. Where do you find your comfort, security, and hope today?

Quotations

Sometimes we are wooed to love by goodness or tenderness or kindness or beauty. Sometimes we are compelled to love by another's need. But we do not love God because we are told to. We love simply "because God first loved us." God started it. And we can't help but respond. It was God who gave us the capacity to love. It is our greatest and most exciting gift, for, at bottom, it is love that creates life. Love is our most God-like quality. We are most like God when we love. (*Faith, the Yes of the Heart*, Brame; p. 29.)

In short, I discovered for myself that one of the major works of prayer is ongoing, over-a-lifetime healing, and some of this healing involves very painful work. One of the monastic teachers was once asked, "Of all the virtues, which is the most difficult to practice?" "It is prayer," he replied, for "prayer is warfare to the last breath." Prayer, I learned, is warfare to the last breath because so much of the healing work of prayer involves gaining knowledge of our own hearts as we strive to understand our actual feelings, attitudes, convictions, and motivations. (*Memories of God*, Roberta C. Bondi; p. 34.)

The notion of unmerited mercy is quaint but unintelligible to most of us, since it has no prototype in our human experience. The dramatic surprise that comes in the stories of the searching shepherd, the searching woman, and the searching father is that being found by a searching God is more important than anything we do. If the message fails to resonate within us, we can't fault the messenger. (*The Wisdom of Tenderness*, Manning; p. 138.)

I do not have to choose between the Sermon on the Mount and the magnolia trees. God can come to me by a still pool on the big island of Hawaii as well as at the altar of the Washington National Cathedral. The House of God stretches from one corner of the universe to the other. Sea monsters and ostriches live in it, along with people who pray in languages I do not speak, whose names I will never know. I am not in charge of this House, and never will be. I have no say about who is in and who is out. I do not get to make the rules. Like Job, I was nowhere when God laid the foundations of the earth. I cannot bind the chains of the Pleiades or loose the cords of Orion. I do not even know when the mountain goats give birth, much less the ordinances of the heavens. I am a guest here, charged with serving other guests—even those who present themselves as my enemies. I am allowed to resist them, but as long as I trust in one God who made us all, I cannot act as if they are no kin to me. There is only one House. Human beings will either learn to live in it together or we will not survive to hear its sigh of relief when our numbered days are done. (*An Altar in the World*, Taylor; pp. 13–14.)

Reflection Time

Making Our Requests Known
Prayer for Our World, Its People and Leaders
Prayer for the Church and Its Leaders

Prayer for Those in Our Circle of Responsibility
Prayer for Ourselves

Offering of Self to God

Prove me, O LORD, and try me;
    test my heart and mind.
For your steadfast love is before my eyes,
    and I walk in faithfulness to you. (Psalm 26:2-3)

Blessing

Now may the God of peace, who brought back from the dead our
Lord Jesus, the great shepherd of the sheep, by the blood of the eternal covenant, make you complete in everything good so that you may
do [God's] will, working among us that which is pleasing in [God's]
sight, through Jesus Christ, to whom be the glory forever and ever.
Amen. (Hebrews 13:20-21)

Week 26

A FAITHFUL WALK

Becoming Aware of God's Presence
You are my God, and I will give thanks to you;
　　you are my God, I will extol you.

O give thanks to the LORD, for he is good,
　　for his steadfast love endures forever. (Psalm 118:28-29)

Inviting God's Intervention
Let your steadfast love come to me, O LORD,
　　your salvation according to your promise. (Psalm 119:41)

Listening for God's Voice

Sunday	*A.* Acts 7:55-60; Psalm 31:1-5, 15-16; 1 Peter 2:2-10; John 14:1-14
	B. Acts 8:26-40; Psalm 22:25-31; 1 John 4:7-21; John 15:1-8
	C. Acts 11:1-18; Psalm 148; Revelation 21:1-6; John 13:31-35
Monday	Luke 16:10-13
Tuesday	Acts 11:19-26
Wednesday	Psalm 119:90-92
Thursday	2 Timothy 4:1-8
Friday	Acts 11:27-30
Saturday	John 17:6-19

Essay
Twenty-five years ago a friend asked me how he should pray for
me as my family and I were preparing to move to another state. I
responded, "Pray that I may be faithful in all things." As soon as I

finished signing a book for him, he wrote my prayer request next to my signature. Recently, we had a wonderful reunion and as we parted he said, "How should I pray for you now that you are retired?" My response was nearly automatic, "Pray that I may remain faithful." He pulled out the well-used *Guide to Prayer* that I had signed twenty-five years ago and opened it to where I had signed and he had written my prayer request. They were the same. My desire for faithfulness then was as intense as my desire for water on a hot summer day. A lot has changed since then. I have seen failure and success, loss and gain, and more times than I wish I have failed to live up to my own prayer and that of my friend. But I can tell you that long years with the same prayer always close to the surface of my mind and heart has led me on a very formative and fulfilling path. It is a path I plan to follow as long as I live. What are your plans?

Quotations

While pursuing the business of the day, we cannot ignore the Spirit-inspired nudges we feel to examine its ups and downs in a prayerful way: "Did I handle this difficult situation as Christ might have done? In what way did my decisions affect others? Did I act out of love for God and them or only for my own gratification?" Allowing God to be as much a part of our ruminations as an intimate friend draws us to deeper union. At the start of the day we ask God for guidance. At the end of the day we replay the tape to see if we have or have not responded wisely. When distractions tap like raindrops against the windowpanes of our mind, we renew our attention and turn toward the Holy. In due time we may experience a deeper calm, a miracle of grace, words fail to convey. (*Late Have I Loved Thee*, Susan Muto; p. 119.)

Drinking the cup that Jesus drank is living a life in and with the spirit of Jesus, which is the spirit of unconditional love. The intimacy between Jesus and Abba, his Father, is an intimacy of complete trust, in which there are no power games, no mutually agreed upon promises, no advance guarantees. It is only love—pure, unrestrained, and unlimited love. Completely open, completely free. That intimacy gave Jesus the strength to drink his cup. That same intimacy Jesus wants to give us so that we can drink ours. That intimacy has a Name, a Divine Name. It is called Holy Spirit. Living a spiritual life is living a life in which the Holy Spirit will guide us and give us the strength and courage to keep saying *yes* to the great question. (*Can You Drink the Cup?* Henri J. M. Nouwen; p. 119.)

Being prayed for is also an element in the life of prayer—a very large part, but often largely underappreciated. When it is Jesus who is praying for us, being prayed for may well be the largest part of prayer. We remember where we are: we are in the John Seventeen Prayer Meeting. Jesus is praying. . . . We are actively listening. We want to be in on what Jesus wills for us, just as we were organically tied into the conversation. We will to be prayerfully present to the praying Presence. We have nothing to say. Jesus, the Word made flesh, is speaking to the Father. He is including us in his prayer. (*Tell It Slant*, Peterson; pp. 217–218.)

The doubt with which we need to temper certainty is a searching doubt. It consists of a perpetual attitude of self-scrutiny, of not being content with the way we are, of poking around behind appearances, and of interrogating ourselves. . . . Maintaining it indicates that we sense eternity's call. To be sure, this doubt can cripple. It can cause us to turn inward too much and make us think that we will never know what our status with God is. It can undermine the delight and adventure that being open to grace brings. It can produce hopelessness both about human nature and about our own ability to elude ambivalence and illusion. In spite of these risks, doubt is necessary, for without it we are not likely to move toward singleness of heart. Though it may seem paradoxical, a childlike faith requires the very thing which, if indulged in, would undermine it. (*Singleness of Heart*, Clifford Williams; p. 139.)

Reflection Time

Making Our Requests Known

Prayer for Our World, Its People and Leaders
Prayer for the Church and Its Leaders
Prayer for Those in Our Circle of Responsibility
Prayer for Ourselves

Offering of Self to God

I have chosen the way of faithfulness;
  I set your ordinances before me.
I cling to your decrees, O LORD;
  let me not be put to shame.
I run the way of your commandments,
  for you enlarge my understanding. (Psalm 119:30-32)

Blessing

Let your steadfast love become my comfort
  according to your promise to your servant.
Let your mercy come to me, that I may live;
  for your law is my delight. (Psalm 119:76-77)

Week 27
ALWAYS IN GOD'S PRESENCE

Becoming Aware of God's Presence
But the Advocate, the Holy Spirit, whom the Father will send in my name, will teach you everything, and remind you of all that I have said to you. (John 14:26)

Inviting God's Intervention
Come Holy Spirit, and do your good and mighty work within and through us this day!

Listening for God's Voice

Sunday	*A.* Acts 17:22-31; Psalm 66:8-20; 1 Peter 3:13-22; John 14:15-21
	B. Acts 10:44-48; Psalm 98; 1 John 5:1-6; John 15:9-17
	C. Acts 16:9-15; Psalm 67; Revelation 21:10, 22–22:5; John 14:23-29
Monday	Romans 8:12-17
Tuesday	1 Corinthians 2:14-16
Wednesday	1 John 2:1-6
Thursday	1 John 2:7-11
Friday	Acts 1:1-5
Saturday	Philippians 1:3-11

Essay
Our hearts race and we are nearly overcome with awe, wonder, and joy when we permit the words of Jesus to even get close to our center of awareness. "Those who love me will keep my word, and my Father will love them, and we will come to them and make our home

with them" (John 14:23b). That God chooses to "live with us" is almost too much for us to comprehend. It takes getting used to. It requires a reordering of our ideas about God and about ourselves. Even as you read these words God is there with you to engage, reveal, guide, comfort, and companion. To remember this truth is to have our lives transformed. To forget it is to risk the danger of falling into fear and anxiety about today and tomorrow. To remember this truth is to face each day, no matter how difficult, or joyful, aware that God's loving and life-giving presence is with us always, and nothing can ever separate us from that presence. Let's remind each other that God has chosen to live with us always as we help each other to live faithfully in the light of that eternal Presence.

Quotations

Jesus' good news about the kingdom can be an effective guide for our lives only if we share his view of the world in which we live. To his eyes this is a God-bathed and God-permeated world. It is a world filled with a glorious reality, where every component is within the range of God's direct knowledge and control—though he obviously permits some of it, for good reasons, to be for a while otherwise than as he wishes. It is a world that is inconceivably beautiful and good because of God and because God is always in it. It is a world in which God is continually at play and over which he constantly rejoices. Until our thoughts of God have found every visible thing and event glorious with his presence, the word of Jesus has not yet fully seized us. (*The Divine Conspiracy*, Willard; pp. 61–62.)

Covenant Prayer is a profound interior heart call to a God-intoxicated life. It leads us to the crossroad of personal decision. It guides us through the valley of sacred commitment. It beckons us up the alpine pathway of holy obedience. The essence of Covenant Prayer is captured in the confession of the Psalmist: "My heart is fixed, O God, my heart is fixed" (Ps. 57:7, KJV). At the altar of

Covenant Prayer we vow unswerving allegiance; we make high resolves; we promise holy obedience. (*Prayer*, Foster; p. 67.)

I need the darkness in order to grow closer to God. Perhaps I am like a night-blooming flower that requires darkness to open my blossoms. In the darkness, I am more fully open to the One who has created me. The darkness has many gifts to offer us if we are willing to enter it. There are painful and scary things in the darkness but there is also creation and rebirth. There is promise and enlightenment. There is transformation and revelation. Most of all, in the darkness we may encounter the God for whom darkness and light are both alike. (*Treasures of Darkness*, Tara Soughers; p. 96.)

To live the life of prayer means to emerge from my drowse, to awaken to the communing, guiding, healing, clarifying, and transforming current of God's Holy Spirit in which I am immersed. But to awaken is not necessarily to return. Awareness, no matter how vivid, must be accompanied by "a longing to dwell with the beauty of His countenance," and until prayer knows, and is the expression of this longing, it is still callow and is likely to melt away at the first sharp thaw. (*Dimensions of Prayer*, Steere; p. 22.)

To adore is to open wide our souls to God who is already there. That is also the beginning of communion. There is communion between God and the individual soul, communion with the Body of Christ as the Communion of Saints, and communion with Christ through the sharing of His Spirit. Underhill notes how we look forward to the spiritual joys and solace of communion, but clearly states that communion also means acceptance of suffering and the Way of the Cross. Yet she reminds us that we are never alone. (From Brame's Introduction to *The Ways of the Spirit*, Underhill; pp. 30–31.)

Reflection Time

Making Our Requests Known
Prayer for Our World, Its People and Leaders
Prayer for the Church and Its Leaders
Prayer for Those in Our Circle of Responsibility
Prayer for Ourselves

Offering of Self to God
We boldly claim the promise of your presence with us and once again offer all that we are and hope to become to be used as you choose, for we are yours.

Blessing
Peace I leave with you; my peace I give to you. I do not give to you as the world gives. Do not let your hearts be troubled, and do not let them be afraid. (John 14:27)

Week 28

JESUS PRAYS FOR OUR UNITY

Becoming Aware of God's Presence

Nevertheless I am continually with you;

you hold my right hand.

You guide me with your counsel,

and afterward you will receive me with honor.

Whom have I in heaven but you?

And there is nothing on earth that I desire other than you.

My flesh and my heart may fail,

but God is the strength of my heart and my portion forever. (Psalm 73:23-26)

Inviting God's Intervention

Give ear, O Shepherd of Israel,

you who lead Joseph like a flock! . . .

Stir up your might,

and come to save us!

Restore us, O God;

let your face shine, that we may be saved. (Psalm 80:1a, 2b-3)

Listening for God's Voice

Sunday	A. Acts 1:6-14; Psalm 68:1-10, 32-35; 1 Peter 4:12-14; 5:6-11; John 17:1-11
	B. Acts 1:15-17, 21-26; Psalm 1; 1 John 5:9-13; John 17:6-19
	C. Acts 16:16-34; Psalm 97; Revelation 22:12-14, 16-17, 20-21; John 17:20-26
Monday	Acts 10:34-36
Tuesday	Luke 9:49-50

Wednesday	Psalm 133
Thursday	Ephesians 3:1-6
Friday	Ephesians 4:1-8
Saturday	1 Peter 1:17-21

Essay

We live in a sharply divided world and there are those who seem to feed on and delight in driving wedges of division wherever they can. We see it in communities and we see it in congregations and denominations. One thing is obvious, and that is that those who seek to drive these wedges of division don't hang around Jesus much. Jesus was not afraid to speak the truth no matter where that truth touched his listeners. But his life was given to heal the wounds of division, and his prayer recorded in John 17 is an emphatic reminder of his determination to see divisions healed and unity restored: "Holy Father, protect them in your name that you have given me, so that they may be one, as we are one" (John 17:11b).

What would our world be like if this prayer of Jesus was answered today? What changes would we see in our communities and our congregations? We do not know all that would happen but we do know that the changes would be dramatic, life-giving, and liberating. Let us pray that the prayer of Jesus will be answered in our time and where we live. And then let us promise God and one another every day that each of us will become a living answer to this fervent prayer of Jesus. It will change our world!

Quotations

Everything that came from Jesus' lips worked like a magnifying glass to focus human awareness on the two most important facts about life: God's overwhelming love of humanity, and the need for people to accept that love and let it flow through them in the way water passes without obstruction through a sea anemone. In experiencing God as infinite love bent on people's salvation, Jesus was an authentic child of Judaism; he differed, we have seen, only in not allowing the post-Exilic holiness code to impede God's compassion. Time after time, as his story of the shepherd who risked ninety-nine sheep to go after the one that had strayed, Jesus tried to convey God's absolute love for every single human being and for everything God has created. . . . If the infinity of God's love pierces to the core of a being, only one response is possible—unobstructed gratitude for the wonders of God's grace. (*The Soul of Christianity*, Smith; pp. 53–54.)

The divine ratification we need is that which comes with the good news that God really does love all people without exception, that God loves "us," and, most importantly, that God loves me! The heart-warming part of the Good News is that we do not have to come to this stunning truth all by ourselves. As we make our efforts to reach out and be open to this loving God, God is already there helping us. This is grace: "I am here; I am with you; I love you; I will never let you go!" (*To Walk Together Again*, Gula; p. 58.)

It is humanity, simply, that is God's focus in earth history, as it must be ours. It is to the world—the entire world—that he gave his Son. And, indeed, in the larger scene it is not even humanity that is his focus, but the entire created cosmos in the context of God's own life. (*The Divine Conspiracy*, Willard; p. 382.)

What we have most in common is not religion but humanity. I learned this from my religion, which also teaches me that encountering another human being is as close to God as I may ever get—in the eye-to-eye thing, the person-to-person thing—which is where God's Beloved has promised to show up. Paradoxically, the point is not to see him. The point is to see the person standing right in front of me, who has no substitute, who can never be replaced, whose heart holds things for which there is no language, whose life is an unsolved mystery. (*An Altar in the World*, Taylor; p. 102.)

Reflection Time

Making Our Requests Known

Prayer for Our World, Its People and Leaders
Prayer for the Church and Its Leaders
Prayer for Those in Our Circle of Responsibility
Prayer for Ourselves

Offering of Self to God

Know that the LORD is God.
> It is he that made us, and we are his;
> we are his people, and the sheep of his pasture.

Enter his gates with thanksgiving,
> and his courts with praise.
> Give thanks to him, bless his name. (Psalm 100:3-4)

Blessing

Bless the LORD, all his hosts,
> his ministers that do his will.
Bless the LORD, all his works,
> in all places of his dominion.
Bless the LORD, O my soul. (Psalm 103:21-22)

Week 29
POWER BEYOND OUR OWN

Pentecost Sunday

Becoming Aware of God's Presence
In the beginning when God created the heavens and the earth, the earth was a formless void and darkness covered the face of the deep, while a wind from God swept over the face of the waters. (Genesis 1:1-2)

Inviting God's Intervention
Sanctify them in the truth; your word is truth. As you have sent me into the world, so I have sent them into the world. (John 17:17-18)

Listening for God's Voice

Sunday	*A.* Acts 2:1-21; Psalm 104:24-34, 35b; 1 Corinthians 12:3b-13; John 20:19-23
	B. Acts 2:1-21; Psalm 104:24-34, 35b; Romans 8:22-27; John 15:26-27; 16:4b-15
	C. Acts 2:1-21; Psalm 104:24-34, 35b; Romans 8:14-17; John 14:8-17, (25-27)
Monday	1 Timothy 4:1-5
Tuesday	1 John 4:1-6
Wednesday	1 Corinthians 3:10-17
Thursday	Joel 2:26-29
Friday	Acts 20:17-24
Saturday	2 Corinthians 1:12-22

Essay
While serving as a District Superintendent I often asked congregations what they were planning for the next year that could not be

accomplished without God's intervention. The Bible is filled with stories of accomplishments that were achieved only as God's people sought, accepted, and invested power from beyond themselves, God's power to achieve their God-honored goals. Far too often we try to do far too much on our own, forgetting that there is help available from the One who made us, loves us, and walks with us in all of life's experiences. Today, instead of getting stressed out because I have too much to do, I will ask God to guide me in my yes and no to tasks and opportunities that come my way. And then I will ask God to inspire, bless, and grant wisdom, energy, and strength beyond my own to do what God has placed in my hands to accomplish. How will you approach the opportunities and tasks that await you?

Quotations

As we enter the community of the resurrection, holy baptism redefines our lives in Trinitarian terms. Baptism is at one and the same time death and resurrection, a renunciation and an embrace. In baptism we are named in the same breath as the Name—Father, Son, and Holy Spirit—and are on our way to understanding our lives comprehensively and in community as children of this three-personed God. We are turned around, no longer going our own way but living as members of the community that follows Jesus. We cannot be trusted to do anything on our own in this business. As Barth insisted so strenuously, we are always beginners with God. (*Christ Plays in Ten Thousand Places*, Peterson; p. 303.)

I believe that prayer is all about our relationship with a God who loves us. Prayer is the way we connect and stay connected to God. We enter into this relationship at the urging of God. God wants an ongoing, vibrant, loving relationship with all of us. God desires us not because we are good or holy or set apart in any way; God calls all of us, just as we are, into relationship and offers us the possibility of intimacy. (*A Praying Congregation*, Vennard; p. 42.)

O Master, let me walk with thee in lowly
paths of service free; tell me thy secret;
help me to bear the strain of toil, the fret of care.

Teach me thy patience; still with thee in closer,
dearer company, in work that keeps faith
sweet and strong, in trust that triumphs over wrong. ("O Master, Let
Me Walk With Thee." Words: Washington Gladden.)

Hope is one of the highest ideals to keep us steady on this walk. It is
what keeps people praying in prison. Hope gives us rest wherever
we are. It assures us that we will be okay, because eventually we are
headed home. We can stand firmly on hope; it's not some lofty, ethereal vision that will leave us when times are rough. It is hope that
kept early faith communities alive during times of persecution, and
it has always been a sign of God's Spirit among us. Hope lives in all
of us and carries us forward when we grow weary. Learning to accept
that gives us power we have never seen. (*Hither and Yon*, Becca
Stevens; p. 130.)

After we have been awakened to the presence of the Spirit, a new
moment arises in our spiritual life. Our effort is now directed to responding to the internal law of the Spirit written in our heart rather
than simply conforming to the external obligations as they have been
presented to us by the authorities in our life. We do indeed continue
to fulfill these obligations, but our reasons have been more deeply
internalized. And responding to the Spirit is a far more challenging
project. It demands that we habitually live in tune with our inner experiences, distinguishing those which flow from the Spirit from those
that do not. [By the term "inner experience"] we simply mean all
those movements that arise within ourselves, such as our memory,
imagination, thinking, feeling, and willing. (*Moving in the Spirit*,
Richard J. Hauser, S. J.; p. 23.)

Reflection Time

Making Our Requests Known
Prayer for Our World, Its People and Leaders
Prayer for the Church and Its Leaders
Prayer for Those in Our Circle of Responsibility
Prayer for Ourselves

Offering of Self to God
With trust and confidence we offer ourselves to you and invite you to bless and use us as you will, for we are yours.

Blessing
God of love, mercy, and peace, pour out your Spirit upon us to form and transform our lives more and more into your grand design for us all.

Week 30
GOD MADE KNOWN

Becoming Aware of God's Presence
For lo, I will come and dwell in your midst, says the LORD. Many nations shall join themselves to the LORD on that day, and shall be my people; and I will dwell in your midst. (Zechariah 2:10b-11)

Inviting God's Intervention
But you, O LORD, do not be far away!
   O my help, come quickly to my aid! (Psalm 22:19)

Listening for God's Voice
Sunday	*A.* Genesis 1:1–2:4a; Psalm 8; 2 Corinthians 13:11-13; Matthew 28:16-20
	B. Isaiah 6:1-8; Psalm 29; Romans 8:12-17; John 3:1-17
	C. Proverbs 8:1-4, 22-31; Psalm 8; Romans 5:1-5; John 16:12-15
Monday	Philippians 2:1-11
Tuesday	Luke 24:44-49
Wednesday	Colossians 1:21-23
Thursday	Isaiah 44:1-8
Friday	Micah 4:1-5
Saturday	John 6:41-51

Essay
Beverly and I met in a college English class taught by a favorite professor. We had known each other for three years when we married and thought we really knew all about each other. Now, fifty-six years later we are still making discoveries about who we are as individuals and about who we are together.

God's introduction (self-disclosure) began when humankind was first created. That self-disclosure has continued and while God is still Mystery, we have come to know God as One, revealed as Father, Son, and Holy Spirit. Much of the Christian community celebrates Trinity Sunday as we continue to try to get to know more fully the One who created all that is, gives us life, redeems us, and chooses to walk with us always to comfort, guide, sustain, defend, and lead us safely to our eternal home. Until that final "Welcome Home," I intend to continue getting acquainted, getting to know, and building a life-giving relationship with the God who has chosen to let us experience Divine Presence every day. What are your intentions?

Quotations

The advantage of believing in the reality of the Trinity is not that we get an A from God for giving "the right answer." Remember, to believe something is to act as if it is so. . . . Hence, the advantage of believing in the Trinity is that we then live as if the Trinity is real: as if the cosmos environing us actually is, beyond all else, a self-sufficing community of unspeakably magnificent personal beings of boundless love, knowledge, and power. And, thus believing, our lives naturally integrate themselves, through our actions, into the reality of such a universe, just as with two plus two equals four. In faith we rest ourselves upon the reality of the Trinity in action—and it graciously meets us. For it is there. And our lives are then enmeshed in the true world of God. (*The Divine Conspiracy*, Willard; p. 318.)

We affirm, we trust, that God has been truthful in God's self-revelation, and that the "faces" of God that we have learned through our experience, and that we have tried to express, however poorly, in our language—first of all in the language of Scripture—show us something of God's own life. From God's work in creation, salvation, and sanctification, we learn something, we think, about the one who creates, saves, and sanctifies. . . . Encountering someone as friend, then as lover, then as partner and comforter, we naturally are moved to reflect on the ways in which these "faces" are not just roles played to suit the circumstances, or masks worn in order to deceive, but dimensions of the other's inner life that were called to outward expression in their relation with us. It is in such a fashion that we, by analogy, try to move carefully from the celebration of the life into which God has caught us up to an appreciation of God's own life. (*The Creed*, Johnson; p. 250.)

Holy Trinity,
Mystery of loving communion,
Invitation to deeper union.
Grant me the grace to pass
The test of trust.
Teach me to be self-donating,
To express freely
A commitment to mutuality,
To ever loving,
Quietly befriending reciprocity.
Strengthen my will to love
My sisters and brothers
As you love us and all others. (*Late Have I Loved Thee*, Muto; p. 23.)

About twenty people sat in a large circle in the lovely fenced-in garden. I tried to explain the mystery of the Trinity by saying that all human relationships are reflections of the relationships within God. God is the Lover, the Beloved, and the Love that binds us in unity. God invites us to be part of that inner movement of love so that we can truly become sons and daughters of the Father, sisters and brothers of the Son, and spouses of the Holy Spirit. Thus, all our human relationships can be lived in God, and as witness to God's divine presence in our lives. (*Sabbatical Journey*, Henri J. M. Nouwen; pp. 177–178.)

If God is sovereign, then we can pray confidently and boldly for the redemption of the world, the conversion of evil to good, the transformation of a timid church to a faithful church, the renewal of a morally bankrupt society to one of justice and mercy and the salvation of our own troubled souls. The God of nature, history, and the Scriptures is sovereign and able to meet any need at any time. Consequently, we are bold enough to pray for God's intervention in today's most difficult problems with the assurance that God is able to transform the weak and timid and to root out even the most deeply entrenched evil. Further, we can invest our energies and direct our lives on the pathway to social and personal holiness because we know that God is with us and is able to help us while defending us and always holding us close. (*A Wesleyan Spiritual Reader*, Job; p. 44.)

Reflection Time

Making Our Requests Known
Prayer for Our World, Its People and Leaders
Prayer for the Church and Its Leaders
Prayer for Those in Our Circle of Responsibility
Prayer for Ourselves

Offering of Self to God
Our soul waits for the LORD;
    he is our help and shield.
Our heart is glad in him,
    because we trust in his holy name.
Let your steadfast love, O LORD, be upon us,
    even as we hope in you. (Psalm 33:20-22)

Blessing
The LORD will keep
    your going out and your coming in
    from this time on and forevermore. (Psalm 121:8)

Week 31
GO WHERE THE WOUNDS ARE

Becoming Aware of God's Presence
You who live in the shelter of the Most High,
  who abide in the shadow of the Almighty,
will say to the LORD, "My refuge and my fortress;
  my God in whom I trust." (Psalm 91:1 2)

Inviting God's Intervention
Remember me, O LORD, when you show favor to your people;
  help me when you deliver them;
that I may see the prosperity of your chosen ones,
  that I may rejoice in the gladness of your nation,
  that I may glory in your heritage. (Psalm 106:4-5)

Listening for God's Voice

Sunday	*A.* Genesis 6:9-22; 7:24; 8:14-19; Psalm 46; Romans 1:16-17; 3:22b-28, (29-31); Matthew 7:21-29
	B. 1 Samuel 3:1-10, (11-20); Psalm 139:1-6, 13-18; 2 Corinthians 4:5-12; Mark 2:23–3:6
	C. 1 Kings 18:20-21, (22-29), 30-39; Psalm 96; Galatians 1:1-12; Luke 7:1-10
Monday	Matthew 11:2-6
Tuesday	Acts 5:12-16
Wednesday	Acts 3:1-10
Thursday	John 9:13-17
Friday	Acts 14:1-7
Saturday	Acts 14:8-18

Essay

Want to follow Jesus? Go where the wounds are, for that is where Jesus went. Demon-possessed, paralyzed, blind, cut off from family and community, ostracized and left out, ridiculed and harassed, divided and estranged, these were the ones who seemed to draw the very presence of Jesus. And not only draw his presence but experience his healing, peace-producing, and life-giving power. Jesus had the ability to show up where the wounds seemed to be greatest and those who heard of him seemed to show up wherever he was to receive the gift of healing.

We don't have to be particularly observant to notice that our world is filled with the wounded and broken. While many of them may feel forgotten, estranged, ridiculed, and left out, they are the very ones to whom Jesus comes to bring healing, hope, and wholeness.

Would you like to experience a new level of effectiveness and faithfulness? Go where the wounds are. This is what Jesus did and that is what Jesus does today. Let's meet him there today and every day and be a part of his life-giving ministry.

Quotations

Jesus was a master communicator. He attracted people who were unaccustomed to his style, ability, and message and connected with them in creative ways. He made difficult concepts vivid and used the language of common people to help point them toward spiritual depth. Yet it was not just clever oratorical skills or provocative stories that enthralled people. It was his drive to connect people with God's heart. (*Unchristian*, Kinnaman and Lyons; p. 210.)

Compassion and a concern for social justice come from the nature of God as seen clearly in Exodus. This is indeed a challenge, for not only are we to hear the cry of those who are suffering in our day but we are also to act for their liberation whenever this is possible. Jesus' instruction, "Be compassionate, as your Father is compassionate" (Luke 6:36, NAB), takes us directly to prayer, for without God's help we could never approach this depth of compassion and care. (*Free to Pray Free to Love*, Olivia; pp. 105–106.)

There is an ethical sharpening that takes place in real Christian prayer that is highly dangerous to any complacency concerning the order of things as they are. The life of Jesus Christ witnessed to God's infinite caring for the very hairs of our heads, and for the lost sheep. It is no accident, therefore, that in prayer, in the presence of Jesus Christ, we are brought inwardly before the revolutionary levelling of God's infinite concern for every soul that comes into the world. "Christianity taught us to care. Caring is the greatest thing—caring matters most." These words of von Hügel's are borne out in Christian prayer; for to come into the field of force of God's infinite caring is to feel inwardly the terrible pull of the unlimited liability for one another that the New Testament ethic lays upon us. This lays the knife at the root of every claim for special privilege and of all "comfortism," and no amount of theological casuistry can justify our disregarding it. (*Dimensions of Prayer*, Steere; p. 106.)

A constant thesis in the writings of Karl Rahner, and indeed of many other great theologians, is that a statement about God is also a statement about ourselves, and vice versa. If we know who is our God and how our God is, then we are well on our way to discerning our own identity. If God is our God, then we are God's people. If our God is a God of life and love, a God who wills freedom, justice, and peace for all, then we must be a people who so live. What God wills to us becomes God's will for us. We must live according to what God intends for us and for all—we must do God's will. This means that to walk humbly with our kind of God, we must walk in solidarity with all people toward the values of God's reign. (*To Act Justly, Love Tenderly, Walk Humbly*, Walter Brueggemann, Sharon Parks, Thomas H. Groome; pp. 54–55.)

Who teaches you? Whose disciple are you? Honestly. One thing is sure: You are somebody's disciple. You learned how to live from somebody else. There are no exceptions to this rule, for human beings are just the kind of creatures that have to learn and keep learning from others how to live. Aristotle remarked that we owe more to our teachers than to our parents, for though our parents gave us life, our teachers taught us the good life. (*The Divine Conspiracy*, Willard; p. 271.)

Reflection Time

Making Our Requests Known
Prayer for Our World, Its People and Leaders
Prayer for the Church and Its Leaders
Prayer for Those in Our Circle of Responsibility
Prayer for Ourselves

Offering of Self to God
O LORD, I am your servant;
    I am your servant, the child of your serving girl.
    You have loosed my bonds.
I will offer to you a thanksgiving sacrifice
    and call on the name of the LORD. (Psalm 116:16-17)

Blessing
The LORD protects the simple;
    when I was brought low, he saved me.
Return, O my soul, to your rest,
    for the LORD has dealt bountifully with you. (Psalm 116:6-7)

Week 32
WHO WILL LEAD US?

Becoming Aware of God's Presence

O LORD, you have searched me and known me.
You know when I sit down and when I rise up;
   you discern my thoughts from far away.
You search out my path and my lying down,
   and are acquainted with all my ways. (Psalm 139:1-3)

Inviting God's Intervention

Hear my prayer, O LORD;
   give ear to my supplications in your faithfulness;
   answer me in your righteousness. (Psalm 143:1)

Listening for God's Voice

Sunday	**A.** Genesis 12:1-9; Psalm 33:1-12; Romans 4:13-25; Matthew 9:9-13, 18-26
	B. 1 Samuel 8:4-11, (12-15), 16-20; (11:14-15); Psalm 138; 2 Corinthians 4:13–5:1; Mark 3:20-35
	C. 1 Kings 17:8-16, (17-24); Psalm 146; Galatians 1:11-24; Luke 7:11-17
Monday	Luke 5:1-11
Tuesday	Mark 1:16-20
Wednesday	Matthew 4:18-22
Thursday	Acts 1:21-26
Friday	Hebrews 3:1-6
Saturday	Luke 18:26-30

Essay

When Jesus chose leaders he went way beyond the normal expectations that observers had assumed would shape the leaders of this new community. Here was the perfect opportunity to shape this new community that would become the church, and Jesus clearly seized the opportunity. His early choice of Matthew shocked the observers. I imagine no one expected Jesus to choose a wealthy tax collector and no one expected that such a person would give up everything and follow Jesus. And the shock waves grew greater when he went to dinner at this tax collector's home. Clearly, Jesus had the capacity to bridge the many, many chasms that were created to keep people apart, ignorant, and suspicious of each other.

I wonder how many times I have missed opportunities to choose leaders as Jesus did. Sometimes I may have been afraid to ask, thinking they would never agree to the radical requirements of the task. And at other times I was afraid to ask because I missed the enormous potential for leadership in persons who could by their very choice bridge chasms that keep people apart and therefore build strong communities of faith and mission. I would like to do better than I did in choosing faithful and effective leaders. How about you?

Quotations

When Jesus deals with moral evil and goodness, he does not begin by theorizing. He plunges immediately (Matt. 5:21-44) into the guts of human existence: raging anger, contempt, hatred, obsessive lust, divorce, verbal manipulation, revenge, slapping, suing, cursing, coercing, and begging. It is the stuff of soap operas and the daily news—and real life. He takes this concrete approach because his aim is to enable people to be good, not just talk about it. He actually knows how to enable people to be good, and he brings his knowledge to bear upon life, as it really is, not some intellectualized and sanctified version thereof. (*The Divine Conspiracy*, Willard; p. 129.)

For a Christian, Jesus is the man in whom it has indeed become manifest that revolution and conversion cannot be separated in man's search for experiential transcendence. His appearance in our midst has made it undeniably clear that changing the human heart and changing human society are not separate tasks, but are as interconnected as the two beams of the cross. Jesus was a revolutionary, who did not become an extremist, since he did not offer an ideology, but Himself. He was also a mystic, who did not use his intimate relationship with God to avoid the social evils of his time, but shocked his milieu to the point of being executed as a rebel. In this sense he also remains for nuclear man the way to liberation and freedom. (*The Wounded Healer*, Nouwen; pp. 20–21).

Integrity . . . it's doing the right thing when we know it's the right thing to do. It's who we are. It's being true to the lives to which we have been called. It's who we are when someone's watching and when there is not a soul in sight. It's called *integrity*. Integrity is vital throughout life. . . . *Personal* integrity is when we are authentically the persons we were created to be. It means living a life of wholeness and congruence. *Moral* integrity is when we do what is right simply because we know it is the right thing to do. It means living a life of character and virtue. Integrity takes both. . . . By my integrity I am defined. Out of that integrity I make the choices that become my life. (*If You Know Who You Are You'll Know What to Do*, Ronald J. Greer; pp. 9–10.)

. . . Integrated leaders *will* help people grow—just by being who they are. They will have no interest in keeping others powerless but instead will be eager to evoke the authority of others and glad to share that evoking task with many colleagues. Saying clearly who they are and where they stand, those leaders will encourage others to do the same, bringing all their experiences and the symbols of the tradition into enlivening conversation. Their integrative skills will also help people bring together many dimensions of their inner lives and find connections between inner life and outer context. Integrated leaders will find creative ways to join many different people's gifts. They will attend to the process, to "the way we are living together here," to the message conveyed by the medium. In this they follow One who called himself the Way (rather than the destination), and made conversations on the road the centerpiece of his leadership training. (*Growing in Authority, Relinquishing Control*, Celia Allison Hahn; p. 174.)

Reflection Time

Making Our Requests Known
Prayer for Our World, Its People and Leaders
Prayer for the Church and Its Leaders
Prayer for Those in Our Circle of Responsibility
Prayer for Ourselves

Offering of Self to God
Every day I will bless you,
    and praise your name forever and ever.
Great is the LORD, and greatly to be praised;
    his greatness is unsearchable. (Psalm 145:2-3)

Blessing
The LORD is gracious and merciful,
    slow to anger and abounding in steadfast love.
The LORD is good to all,
    and his compassion is over all that he has made. (Psalm 145:8-9)

Week 33

WHAT WILL PEOPLE SAY?

Becoming Aware of God's Presence
Make your face shine upon your servant,
   and teach me your statutes. (Psalm 119:135)

Inviting God's Intervention
I have gone astray like a lost sheep; seek out your servant,
   for I do not forget your commandments. (Psalm 119:176)

Listening for God's Voice

Sunday	*A.* Genesis 18:1-15, (21:1-7); Psalm 116:1-2, 12-19; Romans 5:1-8; Matthew 9:35–10:8, (9-23)
	B. 1 Samuel 15:34–16:13; Psalm 20; 2 Corinthians 5:6-10, (11-13), 14-17; Mark 4:26-34
	C. 1 Kings 21:1-10, (11-14), 15-21a; Psalm 5:1-8; Galatians 2:15-21; Luke 7:36–8:3
Monday	Matthew 11:7-19
Tuesday	Luke 15:1-7
Wednesday	Luke 19:1-10
Thursday	Luke 7:31-35
Friday	Galatians 2:11-14
Saturday	Acts 11:1-18

Essay
Jesus got in trouble just by accepting an invitation to share a meal at the home of a Pharisee. But the real trouble began when a woman, identified by the people as a sinner, comes and pours ointment on the feet of Jesus and wipes her tears from his feet with her hair (Luke 7:36-50). It was a remarkable and beautiful act of respect, reverence, gratitude, and affection. But the other guests didn't see it that way.

The response seems to have been, "What's the matter with him? Doesn't he know what kind of woman she is?" Jesus wasn't swayed by the negative response of the other guests, rather he forgives and blesses the woman as he sends her on her way, forgiven and wrapped in the forgiveness of God.

My first appointment out of seminary was to a small congregation in a small town in central North Dakota. This little village had two grocery stores, two hardware stores, two filling stations, two churches, and two bars. One rainy afternoon, I decided to enter one of the bars to speak to one of the members of the congregation whose truck was parked out front. He was not the only member of the congregation present in the bar on that rainy afternoon and, after greeting the rest and completing our brief conversation about a matter at the church, I made my way to other pastoral calls. By the next day, a common topic of conversation was my visit to the bar and being there with "those kind of people." I tried to shrug off the criticism, but it was difficult not to be intimidated by what people were saying. Now, full of years and experience, I wonder how often my footsteps were turned away from "those kind of people" by what people were saying. My prayer today is that I may cultivate the capacity that Jesus demonstrated so clearly and embrace everyone as a child of God, worthy of all the gifts of God, including forgiveness and the opportunity of new beginnings. What is your prayer today?

Quotations

We don't spend much time talking about sin in our culture. We should, however, for sin is real, contagious, and deadly. Unforgiven sin is a burden too heavy for any of us to carry. It leaves little room for joy and assurance in the life of a Christian. Unforgiven sin often lingers in the shadows of our lives, constantly reminding us of our inadequacy, our incompleteness, and our unworthiness. The longer we put off dealing with sin and forgiveness the more difficult it is to receive this free gift of grace. (*A Wesleyan Spiritual Reader*, Job; p. 116.)

It's to the unlikely, the ragged repentant, that Jesus shows up—and revels. It's to those formerly powerless who have every reason to seek and to relish revenge that God gives the greatest power: to forgive. And find a way forward. Forgiveness and mercy help patrol my own heart for being irked or blasé with what Scott Cairns calls

> . . . the annoyance
> of grace, and this tired music
> of salvation. . . .

It helps to keep posted on the marquis [sic] in my mind how deeply in debt I am to forgiveness. (*Why Jesus Makes Me Nervous*, Jordan-Lake; p. 120.)

The law of the universe is that love never dies. It is written deep in the heart of creation and has been translated in many ways in a multitude of times and places. It is voiced by the prophets, telling us to write this law on the hearts of our children. It is preached by the apostles, saying that faith, hope, and love remain when everything else passes. It runs so deeply that people in exile for generations can still dream of love. In all religions, in all times, in all places, love holds humanity in a common good to God. It calls us to love God with all our hearts and minds and bodies, and to love our brothers and sisters as ourselves. (*Hither and Yon*, Stevens; p. 135.)

Forgiveness, however, can only be received by those who will accept its conditions. To be cleansed and to accept cleansing, then to move into the present and the future as a forgiven, a restored one, is the gift of the deepest prayer. The query that might be placed over the door of the Pascalian chamber would be, "Are you willing to accept the forgiveness of God?" (*Dimensions of Prayer*, Steere; pp. 57–58.)

Reflection Time

Making Our Requests Known
Prayer for Our World, Its People and Leaders
Prayer for the Church and Its Leaders

Prayer for Those in Our Circle of Responsibility
Prayer for Ourselves

Offering of Self to God

Let your hand be ready to help me,
    for I have chosen your precepts.
I long for your salvation, O Lord,
    and your law is my delight. (Psalm 119:173-174)

Blessing

I lift up my eyes to the hills—
    from where will my help come?
My help comes from the Lord,
    who made heaven and earth. (Psalm 121:1-2)

Week 34
DO NOT BE AFRAID

Becoming Aware of God's Presence
Say to those who are of a fearful heart,
   "Be strong, do not fear!
Here is your God." (Isaiah 35:4)

Inviting God's Intervention
Hear my prayer, O LORD;
   let my cry come to you.
Do not hide your face from me
   in the day of my distress.
Incline your ear to me;
   answer me speedily in the day when I call. (Psalm 102:1-2)

Listening for God's Voice

Sunday	*A.* Genesis 21:8-21; Psalm 86:1-10, 16-17; Romans 6:1b-11; Matthew 10:24-39
	B. 1 Samuel 17:(1a, 4-11, 19-23), 32-49; Psalm 9:9-20; 2 Corinthians 6:1-13; Mark 4:35-41
	C. 1 Kings 19:1-4, (5-7), 8-15a; Psalm 42 and 43; Galatians 3:23-29; Luke 8:26-39
Monday	Deuteronomy 1:19-21
Tuesday	Joshua 24:14-15
Wednesday	Psalm 56
Thursday	Isaiah 12
Friday	Matthew 8:23-27
Saturday	Philippians 4:4-9

Essay
We live in a fearful and anxious world. The constant bombardment of
24-hour news reports reminding us again and again about disasters,

political infighting, threats from natural causes and those branded as enemies, begins to penetrate our faith and trust in the God we have come to see most clearly in Jesus Christ. And as unnoticed as dusk turning to darkness we easily and suddenly find ourselves in the darkness of fear and anxiety. Is there a way out of this darkness? Is there a way to "live in the light" of God's companionship that wipes away fear and anxiety as surely as the rising sun banishes the darkness of the night? The biblical witness is clear that the answer is, "Yes." And the lives of the saints who have gone before confirm that the biblical response to the question is true and transforming. When the frightened disciples awakened Jesus (Mark 4:38), he quickly calmed the sea and their fears. Today let us remind each other often that the resurrected Jesus no longer needs to be awakened but is a constant companion ready and able to calm our fears and walk with us through all the storms of life that come our way.

Quotations

Jesus looks outward to the cosmos and to the sweep of human history before and after. He tells us we have no need to be anxious, for there is a divine life, the true home of the soul, that we can enter simply by placing our confidence in him: become his friend, and conspiring with him to subvert evil with good. He also shows us how we can be renewed in the depths of our soul, stepping "beyond the goodness of scribes and Pharisees" to become the kinds of persons who are genuinely at home in God's world. (*The Divine Conspiracy*, Willard; p. 215.)

On every page of the Gospels we see how Jesus stretched out his hands of healing, and the sick felt the love of God pour into their broken bodies, minds, and hearts. He was the Son of God and they, for a brief moment, hung suspended between the darkness of their own isolation and the light of the freeing truth that they were sons and daughters of God himself. As they yielded to the presence of Jesus' love in their lives, they felt wholeness come over them. . . . That same living Jesus wishes to pour out his Spirit of love into our hearts; we need only consent to receive this love. He wishes to heal us in the deepest layers of our being, our spirit, from all our haunting and crippling fears by giving us faith to let go of these fears and guilt and all the unnatural reactions that follow and to begin to live in this new life. Through his Holy Spirit he opens our spiritual eyes to his new vision. In this vision we can know through faith, hope, and love that we are really God's children. (*In Jesus We Trust*, Maloney; p. 53.)

As I began to see that darkness as something not to be feared but to be accepted and even embraced, I found others who had shared that experience. Few people talk about embracing the darkness. Far too often Christianity is seen as unending light; only those who have limited faith allow any darkness to creep in. But darkness is just as much a part of our lives as light. God made both the darkness and the light. By denying a place in our faith for darkness, we are limiting the ways in which we can encounter God. I know that my life and my faith have been richer because of the combination of light and darkness. Times of darkness contrast with times of joy, and it is that combination of light and dark that enriches our lives. (*Treasures of Darkness*, Soughers; p. 94.)

The noblest discharge of our responsibility is not in self-management but in abandoning the management to Eternal Wisdom. There is no security that can be won by one's self. There is nothing but security when one's self is given to God. Any part of the self outside of God is in jeopardy. . . . Meaning only God brings us into communion with God and finally to conscious union with Him. It is in such communion and union that an abiding sense of security is born. One has at last reached the Love that will not let one go. In such fellowship there is a final, indestructible certainty. In that certainty is complete confidence as one faces the unknown future, courage in the presence of danger, calm in the midst of recurring crises. We are in His hands and nothing can snatch us away. (*An Autobiography of Prayer*, Albert Edward Day; p. 178.)

Reflection Time

Making Our Requests Known
Prayer for Our World, Its People and Leaders
Prayer for the Church and Its Leaders
Prayer for Those in Our Circle of Responsibility
Prayer for Ourselves

Offering of Self to God
I will sing of loyalty and justice;
    to you, O LORD, I will sing.
I will study the way that is blameless.
    When shall I attain it?

I will walk with integrity of heart
    within my house;
I will not set before my eyes
    anything that is base. (Psalm 101:1-3)

Blessing
Bless the LORD, O my soul,
    and all that is within me,
    bless his holy name.
Bless the LORD, O my soul,
    and do not forget all his benefits—
who forgives all your iniquity,
    who heals all your diseases,
who redeems your life from the Pit,
    who crowns you with steadfast love and mercy,
who satisfies you with good as long as you live
    so that your youth is renewed like the eagle's. (Psalm 103:1-5)

Week 35

TRANSLATING GOOD NEWS INTO GOOD ACTIONS

Becoming Aware of God's Presence

O LORD, you are my God;

I will exalt you, I will praise your name;

for you have done wonderful things,

plans formed of old, faithful and sure. (Isaiah 25:1)

Inviting God's Intervention

I remember the days of old,

I think about all your deeds,

I meditate on the works of your hands.

I stretch out my hands to you;

my soul thirsts for you like a parched land. (Psalm 143:5-6)

Listening for God's Voice

Sunday	*A.* Genesis 22:1-14; Psalm 13; Romans 6:12-23; Matthew 10:40-42
	B. 2 Samuel 1:1, 17-27; Psalm 130; 2 Corinthians 8:7-15; Mark 5:21-43
	C. 2 Kings 2:1-2, 6-14; Psalm 77:1-2, 11-20; Galatians 5:1, 13-25; Luke 9:51-62
Monday	Hebrews 6:1-12
Tuesday	Mark 5:1-12
Wednesday	Luke 6:20-26
Thursday	Hebrews 10:19-25
Friday	Hebrews 10:32-39
Saturday	Luke 6:37-42

Essay

Jesus spent his adult life doing good wherever he was. He seemed to be drawn to the needs and wounds of the world in which he lived his life. His life was truly the gospel; that is good news. The Sunday Gospel readings for this week are reflections of this way of life that left the world better, more whole, and more complete than he found it. It was a radical and risky way of living that is still transforming the world today.

Those who have heard the good news of the gospel and seek to follow Jesus as disciples are invited to live as Jesus did, translating the good news into holy action. It sounds so simple but can be highly challenging, because living the truth of the gospel requires living in fidelity with the gospel. Therefore we cannot ignore the needs of the world, or stand in judgment of those who are not like us. Rather we are compelled by integrity and love to attend to the needs of the world and stand in solidarity with all of God's children, even with those who are not like us. No matter how broken, bruised, confused, and lost, God stands with all, seeking to bring healing, hope, and ultimately bring all safely home. How can we this day translate the gospel into holy action that will join our lives to God's continuous action to transform the world? How will we translate "thy kingdom come, thy will be done" into a way of life?

Quotations

. . . when we see some of our ordinary activities as Christian practices, we come to perceive how *our daily lives are all tangled up with the things God is doing in the world*. Now we want to figure out how to pattern our practices after God's reconciling love for the world. We are never able to do this perfectly, at least not for any length of time. Even so, when we set ordinary daily activities in this context, they are transformed, and so are we. A meal becomes a time of forgiveness. A day of leisure becomes a day of contemplation. An illness turns into an experience of solidarity with the poor. An occupation becomes a vocation. Giving becomes an expression of gratitude. A burial becomes a time of thanksgiving. (*Practicing Our Faith*, Bass; p. 8.)

Holy living carried moral responsibility. John Wesley represented this type of discipleship. He insisted that salvation is ethical throughout and that redemption is a present reality as well as a future hope; that salvation involves the whole life of people and that redemption is realized in community. Several themes have persisted since Wesley's time. There has been a general sensitivity to the corporate bonding of life and an increased awareness of the systemic character of sin. Practical religious activity has served the kingdom of God, a kingdom envisioned as being significantly realized in the concrete conditions of life. Wesleyanism has not thought of the Kingdom in exclusively spiritual terms or as being realized with the church. The Kingdom is found within the actual life the world, and it is to be served in the arena of history. (*Practical Divinity*, Vol. 1, Langford; p. 254.)

In an age of unprecedented brokenness in the life of the individual and growing fractures in the human family, the practice of the Methodist way of Christian living holds great promise for a more faithful personal life and a more just and peaceful world. Could such a practical, simple and yet radical Christianity flourish in our complex, changing, and confusing world? Only if it is tried! . . . Be bold enough to ask God to transform your own life and invest your life as leaven to transform the world where you are. Begin every day in seeking God's direction and companionship, and end every day in offering anew all you have done and all that you are to the One who gives you life. (*A Wesleyan Spiritual Reader*, Job; p. 194.)

If you look at the lives of great pilgrims, most of them had conversion experiences that led them to take radical positions about justice in the world. In many cases, those experiences were the only way the pilgrims would have had the courage and strength to confront powers and principalities in the name of justice or on behalf of those with no power. This is true for us, too. We have to feel the conversion toward right action. This is the place on the journey where I hear my mother's voice call out, "You had better snap out of it." It's time to quit worrying about how it will affect us if we act in accordance with what we believe. It's time to think about how we can live faithfully if we do not act. (*Hither and Yon*, Stevens; p. 80.)

Reflection Time

Making Our Requests Known
Prayer for Our World, Its People and Leaders
Prayer for the Church and Its Leaders
Prayer for Those in Our Circle of Responsibility
Prayer for Ourselves

Offering of Self to God
Teach me to do your will,
    for you are my God.
Let your good spirit lead me
    on a level path. (Psalm 143:10)

Blessing
May the LORD give strength to his people!
    May the LORD bless his people with peace! (Psalm 29:11)

Week 36
CHOSEN AND SENT

Becoming Aware of God's Presence

Happy are those who make
    the LORD their trust,
who do not turn to the proud,
    to those who go astray after false gods. (Psalm 40:4)

Inviting God's Intervention

Be pleased, O LORD, to deliver me;
    O LORD, make haste to help me. (Psalm 40:13)

Listening for God's Voice

Sunday	*A.* Genesis 24:34-38, 42-49, 58-67; Psalm 45:10-17; Romans 7:15-25a; Matthew 11:16-19, 25-30
	B. 2 Samuel 5:1-5, 9-10; Psalm 48; 2 Corinthians 12:2-10; Mark 6:1-13
	C. 2 Kings 5:1-14; Psalm 30; Galatians 6:(1-6), 7-16; Luke 10:1-11, 16-20
Monday	Matthew 12:15-21
Tuesday	Luke 6:12-16
Wednesday	Acts 6:1-6
Thursday	Romans 10:14-17
Friday	Acts 16:6-10
Saturday	Luke 9:1-6

Essay

Sometimes I forget that I did not think of God first, love God first, decide to follow God first, or even decide to permit myself to be sent by God. None of this was my idea at all. It all came from God. Even before I was made, God loved me and had already chosen me. How could I be so arrogant as to think it was my idea all along? Perhaps it was and is my desire to be in charge, to be in control of my own destiny, when deep within I know so very well that I am completely dependent upon God for all things.

I think those first disciples and I have at least that much in common. They were each sought out by God in Christ and had to be reminded who they were, who it was that gave them life and loved them without limit, and who it was that chose them and sent them to be witnesses to the world. Even after three years with Jesus they needed each other and the power of the Holy Spirit to help them remember that they were indeed beloved, chosen, and sent into the world by God. I need as much today. How about you?

Quotations

We are made in the image of God. We look at each person's journey beginning not with original sin but original grace. Our journeys all start and end with God, and everything we do is a step toward our return to wholeness. Because grace is our beginning, we are worthy of all good things. (*Find Your Way Home*, the Women of Magdalene with Becca Stevens; p. 19.)

You do not need to create the possibility of contact with the Spirit. In fact, you cannot create that possibility. For the Holy Spirit is all gift, entirely free. And the gift of the Holy Spirit is none other than the Holy Spirit. Knowing this, being grasped by this uninvited love, moves us to pray. The disciples pleaded with Jesus, "Lord teach us to pray," and Jesus has given us the Spirit to draw us into prayer, to guide us through prayer, to make up for our deficits in prayer, to pray on our behalf when we simply cannot pray. Our challenge is to stop erecting walls that separate us from the Spirit. (*The Kiss of God*, James C. Howell; p. 27.)

Think of yourself as having been sent into the world . . . a way of seeing yourself that is possible if you truly believe that you were loved before the world began . . . a perception of yourself that calls for a true leap of faith! As long as you live in the world, yielding to its enormous pressures to prove to yourself and to others that you are somebody and knowing from the beginning that you will lose in the end, your life can be scarcely more than a long struggle for survival. If, however, you really want to *live* in the world, you cannot look to the world itself as the source of that life. The world and its strategies may help you to survive for a long time, but they cannot help you to live because the world is not the source even of its own life, let alone yours. Spiritually you do not belong to the world. And this is precisely why you are sent into the world. Your family and your friends, your colleagues and your competitors and all the people you may meet on your journey through life are all searching for more than survival. Your presence among them as the one who is sent will allow them to catch a glimpse of the real life. (*Life of the Beloved*, Nouwen; p. 105.)

Evelyn Underhill, writing on courage, speaks of surrender: "However hard we will to be [God's] agents, it doesn't come off that way. It only comes by way of surrender of the whole person to His purposes. And to be able to make that willing surrender, to say yes to God, is the most solemn dynamic of Gethsemane." One of Underhill's recurring themes is that "true Christianity is not all beauty and calm." She writes, "In one form or another, it will involve that awful question [posed by Jesus], 'Can you drink the cup I drink of?' (Matthew 20:22)." The inspiring, exciting side of commitment can easily be lost. One may have to drink "drop by drop out of a tin mug . . . the wine of the surrendered life." (*Faith, the Yes of the Heart*, Brame; p. 165.)

. . . Christian mission is not a matter of announcing something that is foreign to peoples' lives. . . . proclaiming Christ is not similar to informing people that the continent of Australia exists! Rather, it is a matter of bringing to consciousness and making explicit something that is already known implicitly. Like Paul at Athens, the missionary announces the name of the God who has been worshiped without a name. The missionary calls upon people to become aware of who they already are in Jesus Christ. (*Consider Jesus*, Johnson; p. 135.)

Reflection Time

Making Our Requests Known
Prayer for Our World, Its People and Leaders
Prayer for the Church and Its Leaders
Prayer for Those in Our Circle of Responsibility
Prayer for Ourselves

Offering of Self to God
Then I said, "Here I am;
    in the scroll of the book it is written of me.
I delight to do your will, O my God;
    your law is within my heart." (Psalm 40:7-8)

Blessing
By day the LORD commands his steadfast love
    and at night his song is with me,
    a prayer to the God of my life. (Psalm 42:8)

Week 37

WHEN INNOCENTS SUFFER

Becoming Aware of God's Presence
But it is for you, O LORD, that I wait;
  it is you, O Lord my God, who will answer. (Psalm 38:15)

Inviting God's Intervention
Do not forsake me, O LORD;
  O my God, do not be far from me;
make haste to help me,
  O Lord, my salvation. (Psalm 38:21-22)

Listening for God's Voice

Sunday	*A.* Genesis 25:19-34; Psalm 119:105-112; Romans 8:1-11; Matthew 13:1-9, 18-23
	B. 2 Samuel 6:1-5, 12b-19; Psalm 24; Ephesians 1:3-14; Mark 6:14-29
	C. Amos 7:7-17; Psalm 82; Colossians 1:1-14; Luke 10:25-37
Monday	Acts 7:54-60
Tuesday	Acts 8:1-3
Wednesday	Job 21:1-16
Thursday	Job 22
Friday	Zechariah 8:1-8
Saturday	Psalm 112

Essay
The Jesus movement was just getting started when it was shaken by the horrible execution of John the Baptist because of a political grudge. The Gospel reading suggested for this Sunday (Year B) gives the gruesome details and reports on John's disciples' quiet burial of

their leader. This is not the first or the last account of suffering that afflicted the innocent and the faithful. Soon the story of the Jesus movement includes the cruel execution of the Prince of Peace, Jesus, who was the most innocent and faithful of all. We need not look far in our world to see that the innocent still suffer and the faithful are still forsaken by the powers of the world that should defend and protect them.

Thanks be to God that is not the end of the story. For now as then, the darkness cannot put out the light, and now as then, there are those who will stand with and for the suffering innocents. And most of all the promises of God still prevail and our common prayer, "Thy Kingdom Come," is still being answered around the world as multitudes determine to love and serve God and neighbor, regardless of the cost. I want to be included in that community. How about you?

Quotations

Reconciliation must never become an isolated religious phenomenon, or sacramental practice, apart from the daily life of each of us. Just as sin involves multiple relationships, so does reconciliation. . . . Reconciliation involves both God and neighbors. Anyone committed to living a life of reconciliation must attend to the dynamics of love in relationship with God, others, self, and the world. (*To Walk Together Again*, Gula; p. 16.)

Does the point of Christ's suffering get through to people? To some, yes; to others, it does not. Christianity would not have come into being if it hadn't gotten through to St. Paul and the Jesus people, who went about preaching the paradoxical message that Christ crucified *was* the Good News. And it gets through today to Christians who see the church as the family of those who have heard the word of the cross and continue to heed it. (*The Soul of Christianity*, Smith; p. 113.)

I love the simplicity of John's description of Jesus' appearance on that first Easter evening. (See John 20.) . . . The Risen Christ comes quietly and simply stands among his close group of followers. It's like the unobtrusive way he joined those despairing disciples on the road to Emmaus, quietly walking along with them so that they did not realize who he was (see Luke 24:13-35). You have to love the gentle patience of a resurrected Lord who shows up like that! In the upper room that night, Jesus spoke the words those fear-stricken disciples most deeply needed to hear, "Peace be with you" (John 20:19). Then he showed them the marks of the nails in his hands and feet, and the scar from the spear that had ripped open his side. Because of the scars, the disciples knew who he was. (*Strength for the Broken Places*, James A. Harnish; pp. 17–18.)

Praise be to God that our God is a God who enlists us, all of us, to be fellow workers with him, to extend his kingdom of righteousness, to help change the ugliness of this world—its hatred, its enmity, its poverty, its disease, its alienation, its anxiety. He enlists us to be fellow workers with him, to transfigure it into the laughter and the joy, the compassion and the goodness, the love and the peace, the justice and the reconciliation of his kingdom as we work with him to make the kingdoms of this world to become the kingdom of our God and of his Christ. And, hey, the victory is assured! Because the death and resurrection of our Savior Jesus Christ declares forever and ever that light has overcome darkness, that life has overcome death, that joy and laughter and peace and compassion and justice and caring and sharing, all and more have overcome their counterparts. (From *Proceedings of the Fifteenth World Methodist Conference* as quoted in *Strength for the Broken Places*, Harnish; p. 36.)

Reflection Time

Making Our Requests Known
Prayer for Our World, Its People and Leaders
Prayer for the Church and Its Leaders
Prayer for Those in Our Circle of Responsibility
Prayer for Ourselves

Offering of Self to God

I will bless the LORD at all times;
>   his praise shall continually be in my mouth.
My soul makes its boast in the LORD;
>   let the humble hear and be glad.
O magnify the LORD with me,
>   and let us exalt his name together. (Psalm 34:1-3)

Blessing

The salvation of the righteous is from the LORD;
>   he is their refuge in the time of trouble.
The LORD helps them and rescues them;
>   he rescues them from the wicked, and saves them,
>   because they take refuge in him. (Psalm 37:39-40)

Week 38

PRAYER, COMPASSION, AND THE NEEDS OF THE WORLD

Becoming Aware of God's Presence
Open to me the gates of righteousness
    that I may enter through them
    and give thanks to the LORD.

This is the gate of the LORD;
    the righteous shall enter through it.
I thank you that you have answered me
    and have become my salvation. (Psalm 118:19-21)

Inviting God's Intervention
Out of my distress I called on the LORD;
    the LORD answered me and set me in a broad place.
With the LORD on my side I do not fear. (Psalm 118:5-6a)

Listening for God's Voice

Sunday	*A.* Genesis 28:10-19a; Psalm 139:1-12, 23-24; Romans 8:12-25; Matthew 13:24-30, 36-43
	B. 2 Samuel 7:1-14a; Psalm 89:20-37; Ephesians 2:11-22; Mark 6:30-34, 53-56
	C. Amos 8:1-12; Psalm 52; Colossians 1:15-28; Luke 10:38-42
Monday	Psalm 111
Tuesday	Matthew 9:35-38
Wednesday	Matthew 14:13-21
Thursday	Isaiah 55:1-3
Friday	Matthew 15:32-39
Saturday	Romans 12:9-13

Essay

Returning from the mission upon which Jesus had sent them, the disciples were filled with a success story that would make anyone proud and pleased. They poured out their story to Jesus and while he recognized their elation he also recognized their exhaustion and said, "Come away to a deserted place all by yourselves and rest a while" (Mark 6:31). We have all experienced the emotional, physical, and spiritual exhaustion that follows an intense giving of ourselves to a cause greater than we are. Left unattended this exhaustion can be extremely debilitating. So Jesus immediately took the disciples on a retreat. Their boat trip to the place of solitude was a necessary, healing, and life-giving move on the part of Jesus. But once there the compassion of Jesus led him to respond to the needs of the gathered crowd and for the moment to forget the weariness that he and his disciples were carrying. And once again he was teaching and healing as he asked the disciples to give the crowd something to eat.

Prayer, compassion, and the needs of the world are always woven into any faithful life of discipleship. If we are wise we will weave them into a beautiful way of living that brings healing and hope to the world and fulfillment, joy, and peace to ourselves. At this point a word of caution is in order. Jesus had the wisdom to know when time apart was essential and when it was wise to once again engage in ministry. He was clear about resources and about limits. Once again, this is where we as followers must seek and follow the leading and direction that God seeks to bestow.

Quotations

"The time of business," said he, "does not with me differ from the time of prayer; and in the noise and clatter of my kitchen, while several persons are at the same time calling for different things, I possess GOD in as great tranquility as if I were upon my knees at the blessed sacrament." (*The Practice of the Presence of God*, Brother Lawrence; p. 25.)

Christianity began when Jesus emerged from his own wilderness experience to minister to the suffering of an occupied people—occupied not only by Rome but also by the fear that their long oppression meant God had abandoned them. He addressed this fear by healing the sick, feeding the hungry, and freeing those who were possessed by demons, even though his care for other people's pain put him in grave risk of bringing pain upon himself. His death on a Roman cross became both the epitome of human suffering and the proof that even suffering such as that could not force one chosen by God to leave the path of love. (*An Altar in the World*, Taylor; p. 156.)

Jesus' organization was loose and fluid; the most prominent characteristic of the organization was that it didn't have one! No wonder the Romans were puzzled and the chief priests felt threatened. Rather than devote most of his time to administering an organization as our secular world understands it, Jesus spent his time revealing the kingdom of God from within the situations he encountered. If he needed to feed the people, he created a food program (John 6:1-14); if healing was needed, any place could become a clinic (Mark 6:53-56); if teaching was necessary, the world was the classroom (Matt. 5); finally, if a parade was required, a colt or donkey could be borrowed (Matt. 21:2). And just as quickly, all these "organizations" could disappear when they were no longer necessary. Even the great temple might, in theory, be destroyed and rebuilt in three days (John 2:19)! We might call Jesus' administrative style minimalist at best and a type A person's nightmare at worst. (*Leading a Life With God*, Wolpert; p. 141.)

Magdalene is a two-year residential and support community for women coming out of correctional facilities or off the street who have survived lives of abuse, prostitution, and drug addiction. Begun in 1997 in Nashville, Tennessee, Magdalene offers women at no cost a safe, disciplined, and compassionate community in which to recover and rebuild their lives. Magdalene was founded not just to help a subculture of women but to help change the culture itself. The organization stands in solidarity with women who are recovering from sexual abuse, violence, and life on the streets, and who have paid dearly for a culture that buys and sells women like commodities. Magdalene stands as a witness to the truth that in the end, love is more powerful than all the forces that drive women to the streets. (*Find Your Way Home*, the Women of Magdalene with Stevens; p. 111.)

Reflection Time

Making Our Requests Known
Prayer for Our World, Its People and Leaders
Prayer for the Church and Its Leaders
Prayer for Those in Our Circle of Responsibility
Prayer for Ourselves

Offering of Self to God
Your statutes have been my songs
    wherever I make my home.
I remember your name in the night, O LORD,
    and keep your law.
This blessing has fallen to me,
    for I have kept your precepts. (Psalm 119:54-56)

Blessing
Remember your word to your servant,
    in which you have made me hope.
This is my comfort in my distress,
    that your promise gives me life. (Psalm 119:49-50)

Week 39
TEACH US TO PRAY

Becoming Aware of God's Presence

But may all who seek you
   rejoice and be glad in you;
may those who love your salvation
   say continually, "Great is the LORD!"
As for me, I am poor and needy,
   but the Lord takes thought for me.
You are my help and my deliverer;
   do not delay, O my God. (Psalm 40:16-17)

Inviting God's Intervention

As a deer longs for flowing streams,
   so my soul longs for you, O God.
My soul thirsts for God,
   for the living God.
When shall I come and behold
   the face of God? (Psalm 42:1-2)

Listening for God's Voice

Sunday	*A.* Genesis 29:15-28; Psalm 128; Romans 8:26-39; Matthew 13:31-33, 44-52
	B. 2 Samuel 11:1-15; Psalm 14; Ephesians 3:14-21; John 6:1-21
	C. Hosea 1:2-10; Psalm 85; Colossians 2:6-15, (16-19); Luke 11:1-13
Monday	Matthew 7:7-11
Tuesday	Mark 11:20-25
Wednesday	Luke 18:1-8
Thursday	Isaiah 56:6-8

| **Friday** | 2 Corinthians 3:1-6 |
| **Saturday** | 1 John 3:18-24 |

Essay

Three years of face-to-face, in-the-flesh time with Jesus, and it appears that the disciples asked him to teach them only one thing. They must have known there was much they did not know about being a disciple and bearing witness to the gospel. And yet, they asked Jesus to teach them just one thing: how to pray. Was it because it was such a difficult thing to learn how to pray? Or, was it that they saw it was the essential practice, the center of power, the ultimate source of companionship, the connection to the loving Abba that Jesus loved, listened to, and obeyed? I believe it was the latter, and the disciples wanted what Jesus had and wanted to be like Jesus and wanted to live like Jesus. And they could see that there was only one way to receive that gift, and it was through prayer. So the one thing they asked Jesus to teach them was to pray. Jesus promised the Spirit would teach us everything we need to know (John 14:26), and Paul confirms the Spirit's assistance as we pray (Romans 8:26). And so today we pray the prayer Jesus taught us and try to follow its themes in our own prayers and still we ask, as did those first disciples, "Teach us to pray." Because we too want to stay connected to our divine Abba and live as Jesus lived.

Quotations

As you begin to explore your own prayer life and if you are called on to guide others in becoming part of a praying congregation, a good place to begin is with how you learned to pray. Those early lessons, whether in childhood or later, are the foundation on which your present prayer life rests. You many not have thought about learning to pray or even many not recall how you were taught or who taught you to pray. But somewhere in your history, someone introduced you to God. Do you know who it was? (*A Praying Congregation*, Vennard; p. 23.)

I can promise that you will meet Christ in daily prayer, in festal celebrations around the year, in the experience and remembrance of baptism, and in the celebration of the Eucharist. When Jesus talks with his disciples about how to handle fractures in the church, he concludes with this promise: "For where two or three are gathered in my name, I am there among them" (Matt. 18:20). I read that as both a promise and a yearning. The risen Christ yearns to be among us as a community of shared discipline and grace-filled worship. He promises to be present around font, book, and table. Your part is to include yourself in that community of open hands, hearts, and minds for the sake of Love. (*Patterned by Grace*, Benedict; pp. 19–20.)

We today yearn for prayer and hide from prayer. We are attracted to it and repelled by it. We believe prayer is something we should do, even something we want to do, but it seems like a chasm stands between us and actually praying. We experience the agony of prayerlessness. We are not quite sure what holds us back. . . . But for now there is one "something" that needs immediate attention. It is the notion—almost universal among us modern high achievers—that we have to have everything "just right" in order to pray. . . . Our problem is that we assume prayer is something to master the way we master algebra or auto mechanics. That puts us in the "on-top" position, where we are competent and in control. But when praying, we come "underneath," where we calmly and deliberately surrender control and become incompetent. "To pray," writes Emilie Griffin, "means to be willing to be naïve." (*Prayer*, Foster; pp. 7–8.)

Whatever else it may be, prayer is first and foremost an act of love. . . . Jesus prayed primarily because he loved his Father. . . . His personal experience of Yahweh Sabaoth as loving Father shaped not only his self-understanding but, like a knife slashing through wallpaper, brought a dramatic breakthrough into undreamed-of intimacy with God in prayer. Childlike candor, boundless trust, easy familiarity, deep reverence, joyful dependence, unflagging obedience, unmistakable tenderness, and an innate sense of belonging characterized

Jesus' prayer. (*A Glimpse of Jesus: The Stranger to Self-Hatred*, Brennan Manning; pp. 83–84.)

Reflection Time

Making Our Requests Known
Prayer for Our World, Its People and Leaders
Prayer for the Church and Its Leaders
Prayer for Those in Our Circle of Responsibility
Prayer for Ourselves

Offering of Self to God
I trust in the steadfast love of God
    forever and ever.
I will thank you forever,
    because of what you have done.
In the presence of the faithful
    I will proclaim your name, for it is good. (Psalm 52:8b-9)

Blessing
Save me, O God, by your name,
    and vindicate me by your might.
Hear my prayer, O God;
    give ear to the words of my mouth. (Psalm 54:1-2)

Week 40
GUARDING AGAINST GREED

Becoming Aware of God's Presence

The heavens are telling the glory of God;
    and the firmament proclaims his handiwork.
Day to day pours forth speech,
    and night to night declares knowledge.
There is no speech, nor are there words;
    their voice is not heard;
yet their voice goes out through all the earth,
    and their words to the end of the world. (Psalm 19:1-4)

Inviting God's Intervention

O send out your light and your truth;
    let them lead me;
let them bring me to your holy hill
    and to your dwelling. (Psalm 43:3)

Listening for God's Voice

Sunday	**A.** Genesis 32:22-31; Psalm 17:1-7, 15; Romans 9:1-5; Matthew 14:13-21
	B. 2 Samuel 11:26–12:13a; Psalm 51:1-12; Ephesians 4:1-16; John 6:24-35
	C. Hosea 11:1-11; Psalm 107:1-9, 43; Colossians 3:1-11; Luke 12:13-21
Monday	Matthew 19:16-22
Tuesday	Matthew 19:23-26
Wednesday	Jeremiah 6:13-16
Thursday	1 Timothy 6:17-19
Friday	2 Peter 2:1-3
Saturday	Matthew 19:27-30

Essay

The world is being rocked and shaken by the most severe economic crisis in nearly 80 years. Finger pointing and blame assignment have become daily pastimes. Who started this incredible shrinking of the world's wealth? Who was most greedy in this global picture of greed? Jesus clearly identifies the danger and foolishness of greed in the parable of the rich fool (Luke 12:13-21). But could it be that Jesus is also teaching about the wisdom of living a life of radical trust in the One who loves us beyond our comprehension rather than trust in what we can accumulate and call "mine"? I want to move more completely into that radical trust area where I see all things as belonging to God and available to all God's children as I try to forsake the greed that labels all I can accumulate as mine and blinds my eyes to the goodness God intends for me and for all of God's beloved children. Shall we try to walk this way of trust together? It will be so much easier than trying to walk it alone.

Quotations

The dream of Jesus Christ is the Kingdom of God, and the committed Christian buys into his dream. It ought to be noted that the Kingdom is not an abstraction. It is a concrete, visible, and formidable reality forged by the personal commitment of many members. A commitment that does not issue in humble service, suffering discipleship, and creative love is an illusion. The world has no interest in abstractions, and Jesus Christ is impatient with illusions. (*A Glimpse of Jesus*, Manning; p. 104.)

The journey of discovering what we're born for seems first to lead us to death. That is not a hopeless place, though. I suspect from it will emerge some clue about what—or whom—we'd be willing to die for. For from the cold stone of a threatened life we instinctively venture back to the fire, the one that warms us and keeps our blood moving. (*Woman Overboard*, Jo Kadlecek; p. 79.)

Those who have gone before us along the pathway of discernment, seeking only God's will and way, remind us that dissatisfaction with things as they are is one essential element in discovering God's will. When we are settled and very comfortable, it is hard to listen for and respond to God's voice calling us to move out, over, up, beyond, or even to new ministry where we are. (*A Guide to Spiritual Discernment*, Job; p. 36.)

Prayer is strange in being an activity where no success is possible. There is no perfect prayer—except insofar as it corresponds to one's real situation and represents a total turning toward God. The ecstatic prayer of a mystic is in no way superior to the agonized stumbling of a sinner weighed down with guilt and deformed by a lifetime of estrangement from God. Both attempts represent the upward striving of created nature to find rest in God; both are real, both are "successful." Both remain imperfect, too, because perfection does not belong in this life; it is to be expected in the next. (*Toward God*, Casey; p. 24.)

This is important: prayer isn't when we grit our teeth and embrace an unpleasant life. Instead, prayer is when we discover what a truly pleasant life is—and true happiness is not won through addictions to greed, lust, sloth, and envy. Through the eyes of faith we see that sin is the most self-destructive thing imaginable. There is a deeper kind of selfishness that says, "The absolute best thing I can do for myself and for others, is to praise and serve God." (*The Beautiful Work of Learning to Pray*, James C. Howell; pp. 64–65.)

One of the wonders of the world is the rampant sin that flourishes to applause in Christian communities and organizations. Ambition and pride and avarice are uncritically given places of honor and then "supported" with a proof text and sealed with prayer. Jesus is not an uncritical prayer-answerer. He has been through this before. Those forty days and nights of desert temptation allowed no room for naiveté in these matters. Everything that the devil put before Jesus was wrapped in Scripture packaging. Jesus was not tempted by the obvious evil but by the apparent good. He saw through it and stood fast. And now he sees through this man's so very correct prayer—and stands fast. . . . (Luke 12:13-21) (*Tell It Slant*, Peterson; pp. 58–59.)

Reflection Time

Making Our Requests Known
Prayer for Our World, Its People and Leaders
Prayer for the Church and Its Leaders
Prayer for Those in Our Circle of Responsibility
Prayer for Ourselves

Offering of Self to God
Then I will go to the altar of God,
    to God my exceeding joy;
and I will praise you with the harp,
    O God, my God. (Psalm 43:4)

Blessing
Let the words of my mouth and the meditation of my heart
    be acceptable to you,
    O LORD, my rock and my redeemer. (Psalm 19:14)

Week 41
GOD'S PLEASURE

Becoming Aware of God's Presence

Happy are those
   who do not follow the advice of the wicked,
or take the path that sinners tread,
   or sit in the seat of scoffers;
but their delight is in the law of the LORD,
   and on his law they meditate day and night. (Psalm 1:1-2)

Inviting God's Intervention

Why, O LORD, do you stand far off?
   Why do you hide yourself in times of trouble?
In arrogance the wicked persecute the poor—
   let them be caught in the schemes they have devised. (Psalm 10:1-2)

Listening for God's Voice

Sunday	**A.** Genesis 37:1-4, 12 28; Psalm 105:1-6, 16-22, 45b; Romans 10:5-15; Matthew 14:22-33
	B. 2 Samuel 18:5-9, 15, 31-33; Psalm 130; Ephesians 4:25–5:2; John 6:35, 41-51
	C. Isaiah 1:1, 10-20; Psalm 50:1-8, 22-23; Hebrews 11:1-3, 8-16; Luke 12:32-40
Monday	Matthew 6:25-33
Tuesday	Romans 14:13-23
Wednesday	Matthew 3:1-6
Thursday	Galatians 4:1-7
Friday	Ephesians 2:1-10
Saturday	1 Peter 4:7-11

Essay

What could possibly give God pleasure? We might ask every good parent the same question and in their answers find some insight into one of our Sunday Gospel readings that declares that it is God's "good pleasure" to give us the kingdom of God (Luke 12:32). Perhaps the church (little flock) then was as anxious about the events of the times as we are today. The kingdom for which Jesus taught them to pray often seemed so distant and the path toward it so dangerous that fear and anxiety could have easily robbed them of confidence, hope, and joy. But Jesus reminds them that the Sovereign God finds great pleasure in ushering in the Kingdom on earth as it is in heaven and giving it all to the children of God.

What is it in God's kingdom that you most desire? Peace? Presence? Plenty for all? Greater faith and fidelity in the world, the church, and in your own life? Certainly these are some of the gifts of the Kingdom that God is pleased to bestow on the whole creation and each of us. What would happen if we claim them for ourselves and offer them to the world today? Let's try it and see!

Quotations

Here is the God I want to believe in: a Father who, from the beginning of creation, has stretched out his arms in merciful blessing, never forcing himself on anyone, but always waiting; never letting his arms drop down in despair, but always hoping that his children will return so that he can speak words of love to them and let his tired arms rest on their shoulders. His only desire is to bless. (*The Return of the Prodigal Son*, Henri J. M. Nouwen; pp. 93–94.)

I'd like to say something a bit different about prayer, and therefore about religion. Prayer is not primarily saying words or thinking thoughts. It is, rather, a stance. It's a way of living in the Presence. It is, further, a way of living in awareness of the Presence, even enjoying the Presence. The full contemplative is not just aware of the

Presence, but trusts, allows, and delights in it. (*Everything Belongs*, Rohr; p. 29.)

Until I become truly aware of the world in which I live, I cannot possibly get more out of a situation than a mere outline of reality, a kind of caricature of time. It takes a lifetime to really understand that God is in what is standing in front of me. Most of life is spent looking, straining to see the God in the mist, behind the cloud, beyond the dark. It is when we face God in one another, in creation, in the moment, that the real spiritual journey begins. Everything in life is meant to stretch me beyond my superficial self to my better self, to the Ultimate Good who is God. But before that can happen, I must be alive in it myself. I must ask of everything in life: What is this saying to me about life? (*Illuminated Life*, Joan Chittister; p. 24.)

This book is written to help you explore this "many-splendored" heart of God. It is not about definitions *of* prayer or terminology *for* prayer or arguments *about* prayer, though all of these have their place. Nor is it about methods and techniques of prayer, though I am sure we will discuss both. No, this book is about a love relationship: an enduring, continuing, growing love relationship with the great God of the universe. And overwhelming love invites a response. Loving is the syntax of prayer. To be effective pray-ers, we need to be effective lovers. In "The Rime of the Ancient Mariner," Samuel Coleridge declares, "He prayeth well, who loveth well." Coleridge, of course, got this idea from the Bible, for its pages breathe the language of divine love. Real prayer comes not from gritting our teeth but from falling in love. (*Prayer*, Foster; p. 3.)

Reflection Time

Making Our Requests Known
Prayer for Our World, Its People and Leaders
Prayer for the Church and Its Leaders

Prayer for Those in Our Circle of Responsibility
Prayer for Ourselves

Offering of Self to God
Protect me, O God, for in you I take refuge.
I say to the LORD, "You are my Lord;
    I have no good apart from you."

As for the holy ones in the land, they are the noble,
    in whom is all my delight. (Psalm 16:1-3)

Blessing
You show me the path of life.
    In your presence there is fullness of joy;
    in your right hand are pleasures forevermore. (Psalm 16:11)

Week 42
LOVE TRUMPS DIVISION

Becoming Aware of God's Presence

O LORD, who may abide in your tent?
   Who may dwell on your holy hill?

Those who walk blamelessly, and do what is right,
   and speak the truth from their heart;
who do not slander with their tongue,
   and do no evil to their friends,
   nor take up a reproach against their neighbors . . . (Psalm 15:1-3)

Inviting God's Intervention

Rise up, O LORD; O God, lift up your hand;
   do not forget the oppressed.
Why do the wicked renounce God,
   and say in their hearts, "You will not call us to account"? (Psalm 10:12-13)

Listening for God's Voice

Sunday	*A.* Genesis 45:1-15; Psalm 133; Romans 11:1-2a, 29-32; Matthew 15:(10-20), 21-28
	B. 1 Kings 2:10-12; 3:3-14; Psalm 111; Ephesians 5:15-20; John 6:51-58
	C. Isaiah 5:1-7; Psalm 80:1-2, 8-19; Hebrews 11:29–12:2; Luke 12:49-56
Monday	John 7:40-44
Tuesday	Micah 7:1-7
Wednesday	Matthew 10:34-39
Thursday	Matthew 5:43-48
Friday	1 Corinthians 4:8-13
Saturday	Luke 6:27-36

Essay

We live in a divisive and violent world. While division, conflict, and violence are as old as Genesis, they are also as new and troubling as the current religious conflicts and the latest violence of word and act. There is near universal agreement that the way of division and violence is destructive and can never usher in the Kingdom for which Jesus taught us to pray. And yet we seem unable to incorporate the full range of Jesus teaching about the futility of any other way than the way of love. Jesus was clear that his message and he himself would push individuals to decide and choose whom they would follow. But his message was clear: Love always trumps violence and division. For love always draws us toward one another and toward God, and violence always separates us and moves us away from God as we move away from the chosen way of life that Jesus modeled and taught.

In my better moments I always want to bring reconciliation, unity, and peace to every community of which I am a part. And when I become too frightened by the risk of doing so I remember that Jesus demonstrated that love always trumps violence and division. So I pray for grace to always play the trump card God has given. How about you?

Quotations

I belong to God: We do not project or generate grace. Nor do we initiate the redemptive order—process—which, when we let it, sweeps into its course our scarred lives, our prayers, and our concerns for others. . . . The redemptive process is already going on. It sprang out of the heart of the Creator of nature; it is a kind of second creation. It is directed to free souls who, in spite of belonging to God and owing all to God, are yet free to reject and repulse [God's] costly advances. There is a company of the redeemed, a communion of faithful souls, both living and dead, who join with Christ and the Father in laying siege to the heart of the world. The cross is the symbol of the costly caring of this second creation, of this redemptive love. (*Dimensions of Prayer*, Steere; pp. 14–15.)

It is in the New Testament that *shalom* becomes a reality that is not only primordial and eschatological but existential. *The heart of the New Testament message is that the radical possibility of peace has entered our world in Jesus Christ.* In a remarkable passage in Ephesians (2:11-22), Paul says Jesus Christ *is* our peace. He has broken down the dividing wall, the hostilities that have separated us; for he has made both of us into one. When Paul spoke of Christ making the two of us one, he spoke of only the world he knew: one divided into Jesus and Gentiles. He could not have known the full import of his words. Jesus came to break down the barriers that separate all peoples, not just Jews and Gentiles. He is the one who comes to reconcile the First World with the Second World and the Third World. Paul could never have expressed it in that way; even you and I could not have expressed it that way even a few decades ago. (*Seeds of Peace*, William H. Shannon; pp. 108–109.)

Jesus called his disciples to the impossible: "Love your enemies; do good to those who hate you; speak well of those who speak evil of you; pray for those who persecute you." (Lk 6) Yes, this is the impossible love that Jesus comes to announce in order that humanity work towards unity. This way of non-violence, forgiveness, and reconciliation, of acceptance of people who are different . . . will shake all the foundations of societies closed in upon themselves. . . . It will be a new force given by Jesus in love where hate is transformed into forgiveness and enemies into friends. This transformation will take time, for the Kingdom grows little by little like a seed; it is founded on love and on communion. (*Jesus, the Gift of Love*, Jean Vanier; pp. 96–97.)

Perhaps the most essential characteristic of our spiritual life is expressed in offering one another unconditional acceptance as persons. This does not mean accepting destructive behavior, but learning to communicate complete acceptance of the other as a person with no strings attached. Unconditional love is always an expression of God's love. To love in God's way involves generous self-giving. A vital family life requires a great deal of give and take—the capacity for compromise, yielding to others, and graciously being yielded to. We find it hard to give ourselves freely to others when we are judging them. I speak of judgment here in the sense of condemnation rather than of discernment. The condemning face of judgment is a form of withholding personal acceptance, thus a way of withholding the self. . . . When we stand firmly on the ground of unconditional acceptance, mutual commitment, and encouragement, we are in a position to confront one another with needed challenges out of a posture of love. Paul calls this spiritual art "speaking the truth in love" (Eph. 4:15). It is truly a demanding skill, beginning with the discipline of discerning what is true and following with the capacity both to offer authentic appreciation when fitting and to confront gently yet firmly when needed. . . . The deceptively simple phrase, "speaking the truth in love," clearly indicates that the *spirit* in which one speaks truth is as important as the truth one speaks. (*Family: The Forming Center*, Marjorie J. Thompson; pp. 59, 61.)

Reflection Time

Making Our Requests Known
Prayer for Our World, Its People and Leaders
Prayer for the Church and Its Leaders
Prayer for Those in Our Circle of Responsibility
Prayer for Ourselves

Offering of Self to God
O guard my life, and deliver me;
    do not let me be put to shame, for I take refuge in you.
May integrity and uprightness preserve me,
    for I wait for you. (Psalm 25:20-21)

Blessing
The friendship of the LORD is for those who fear him,
    and he makes his covenant known to them. (Psalm 25:14)

Week 43
WHOM SHALL WE FOLLOW?

Becoming Aware of God's Presence
How lovely is your dwelling place,
    O LORD of hosts!
My soul longs, indeed it faints
    for the courts of the LORD;
my heart and my flesh sing for joy
    to the living God. (Psalm 84:1-2)

Inviting God's Intervention
O LORD God of hosts, hear my prayer;
    give ear, O God of Jacob!
Behold our shield, O God;
    look on the face of your anointed.

For a day in your courts is better
    than a thousand elsewhere. (Psalm 84:8-10a)

Listening for God's Voice

Sunday	*A.* Exodus 1:8–2:10; Psalm 124; Romans 12:1-8; Matthew 16:13-20
	B. 1 Kings 8:(1, 6, 10-11), 22-30, 41-43; Psalm 84; Ephesians 6:10-20; John 6:56-69
	C. Jeremiah 1:4-10; Psalm 71:1-6; Hebrews 12:18-29; Luke 13:10-17
Monday	Luke 9:57-62
Tuesday	Matthew 8:18-22
Wednesday	1 John 2:26-29
Thursday	1 John 3:1-4

| **Friday** | John 10:1-4 |
| **Saturday** | John 10:22-30 |

Essay

Many people were offended. They just could not believe what Jesus was saying. "It is the spirit that gives life; the flesh is useless. The words I have spoken to you are spirit and life" (John 6:63). As quickly as they turned toward Jesus, they now turned away. Because so many turned away Jesus turned to the twelve and gave them opportunity to go with the crowd. "Do you also wish to go away?" Jesus asked (verse 67). He was very aware of the pressure that culture, country, and religion were exerting on all who lived in such a troubled time and place. So now the chosen ones are given the opportunity to make their own choice. As you might expect, Peter was the first to speak. "Lord, to whom can we go? You have the words of eternal life. We have come to believe and know that you are the Holy One of God" (6:68b-69). After watching the crowd walk away, and considering the options, they chose to follow Jesus.

Many are still offended today by the company Jesus keeps, by the words he speaks and the invitation he continually gives to follow up close and to become as engaged with life in this troubled time and place as he is. And very likely we will have opportunity every day to choose to follow Jesus or turn away in offense or fear. I am praying for grace and strength to respond something like Peter did. What are you praying for today?

Quotations

Consider it like this. You have offered yourselves, one way or another, to try to work for God. You want, as it were, to be one among the sheepdogs employed by the Good Shepherd. Now have you ever watched a good sheepdog at his work? He is not at all an emotional animal. He just goes on with his job quite steadily, takes no notice of bad weather, rough ground, or his own comfort. He seldom or never comes back to be stroked. Yet his faithfulness, his intimate understanding with his master, is one of the loveliest things in the world. Now and then he just looks at the shepherd. When the time comes for rest they can generally be found together. Let this be the model of our love. (*The Ways of the Spirit*, Underhill; p. 62.)

There is a providence of God active in the life of every person. This is no blueprint which once settled cannot be changed. It is a patient, paternal, infinitely loving willingness to provide a way from wherever we are to our Father's house. If we are off course or going backward or completely stationary, a way can still be plotted. There is always a way. To put ourselves outside the providence of God would be like falling off the edge of the earth. (*Toward God*, Casey; p. 4.)

The difference the gospel of Jesus makes in the here and now is not that "things get better," but that we do. In their letters, both Peter and Paul make the connection between what God has become and done for us in Jesus Christ and what we disciples ourselves are now to become and do for God in his Son. Toward the end of his second letter, Peter writes of the second coming of Jesus, saying, "what sort of persons ought [you] to be, conducting yourselves in holiness and devotion" (2 Peter 3:11). What does God call us disciples to do and become, for him and for one another, in response to the good news of the kingdom? From the beginning, Christians have been idealists. Jesus constantly calls us to strive toward the ideal of being perfected "as your heavenly Father is perfect" (Matthew 5:48). We are to strive toward ideals that we most likely will never achieve, but the striving is what matters. We are to strive joyously, confidently, perseveringly, trusting in grace and not in a neurotic perfectionism that gives way to discouragement or bitterness. The silver may never be without its tarnish, but the polishing makes it shine. (*Precious as Silver: Imagining Your Life With God*, George H. Niederauer; p. 78.)

Jesus reminds us that prayer is a little like children coming to their parents. Our children come to us with the craziest requests at times! Often we are grieved by the meanness and selfishness in their requests, but we would be all the more grieved if they never came to us even with their meanness and selfishness. We are simply glad that they do come—mixed motives and all. This is precisely how it is with prayer. We will never have pure enough motives, or be good enough, or know enough in order to pray rightly. We simply must set all these things aside and begin praying. In fact, it is in the very act of prayer itself— the intimate, ongoing interaction with God—that these matters are cared for in due time. (*Prayer*, Foster; p. 8.)

Reflection Time

Making Our Requests Known
Prayer for Our World, Its People and Leaders
Prayer for the Church and Its Leaders
Prayer for Those in Our Circle of Responsibility
Prayer for Ourselves

Offering of Self to God
I would rather be a doorkeeper in the house of my God
    than live in the tents of wickedness. (Psalm 84:10b)

Blessing
Even the sparrow finds a home,
    and the swallow a nest for herself,
    where she may lay her young,
at your altars, O LORD of hosts,
    my King and my God. . . .

Happy are those whose strength is in you . . . (Psalm 84:3, 5a)

Week 44
WHERE SHALL WE SIT?

Becoming Aware of God's Presence

Praise the LORD, all you nations!
    Extol him, all you peoples!
For great is his steadfast love toward us,
    and the faithfulness of the LORD endures forever.
Praise the LORD! (Psalm 117)

Inviting God's Intervention

I love the LORD, because he has heard
    my voice and my supplications.
Because he inclined his ear to me,
    therefore I will call on him as long as I live. (Psalm 116:1-2)

Listening for God's Voice

Sunday	*A.* Exodus 3:1-15; Psalm 105:1-6, 23-26, 45c; Romans 12:9-21; Matthew 16:21-28
	B. Song of Solomon 2:8-13; Psalm 45:1-2, 6-9; James 1:17-27; Mark 7:1-8, 14-15, 21-23
	C. Jeremiah 2:4-13; Psalm 81:1, 10-16; Hebrews 13:1-8, 15-16; Luke 14:1, 7-14
Monday	Matthew 23:1-12
Tuesday	1 Peter 5:1-5
Wednesday	Psalm 18:27-33
Thursday	James 4:1-6
Friday	Matthew 19:16-22
Saturday	Luke 16:14-15

Essay

Jesus was invited to a dinner at the home of a religious leader and noticed the rush of many of the guests to get to the head table. He also noticed that those invited all seemed to be well connected, religious leaders, family members, or wealthy neighbors. The Pharisees were watching Jesus to see how he would respond to what they saw as a compromising situation. Once again Jesus rose to the occasion and told a parable about humility and hospitality that must have shocked and shamed the dinner guests (Luke 14:1-14). Jesus was often found in the homes of, and at dinner with, those who were rejected by the religious leaders of his time. He refused to live by artificial distinctions set up to isolate, elevate, or denigrate anyone. He saw each person as a child of God, deeply loved and made worthy by his or her creation by the Creator of all that exists.

The tendency continues even today to separate and classify individuals into categories that are often negative and demeaning. In our honest moments we confess that we too have bought into this system that says the head table is the place to be. And there are those who watch the followers of Jesus to see how they respond to these artificial categories that separate, denigrate, and elevate persons and divide the human family in unhealthy ways. Will we buy into the system and philosophy that says I want and deserve the best seat in the house? Or, will we really follow Jesus and take the poorest seat because we see everyone as worthy to sit at the head of the table as we are? Let's pray for the necessary grace to always choose the way of Jesus rather than the way of the world.

Quotations

Those who forget themselves must, of course, also forget that they are doing so. For once the thought that they are forgetting themselves slips into their consciousness, they are liable to congratulate themselves for it. Self-forgetfulness, it should be noted, is not just disregarding ourselves; it is also focusing attention on something outside us. . . . Worship works in the same way, and so does gratitude for God's love. Self-forgetful gratitude has God as its object, not the gratitude itself. Once the gratitude becomes the focus of attention, the temptation to congratulate ourselves arises. . . . The self-forgetful person, Kierkegaard tells us, thinks of the sufferings of others, their troubles and pains, and their struggles and losses. She rejoices in their joys and delights in their virtues and accomplishments. She does not insist that people notice her, nor does she insist that she notice herself. Her noticing is centered elsewhere. (*Singleness of Heart*, Williams; pp. 42–43.)

In the examen of conscience we are inviting the Lord to search our hearts to the depths. Far from being dreadful, this is a scrutiny of love. . . . Without apology and without defense we ask to see what is truly in us. It is for our own sake that we ask these things. It is for our good, for our healing, for our happiness. I want you to know that God goes with us in the examen of conscience. It is a joint search, if I may put it that way. This fact is helpful for us to know for two equally important but opposite reasons. To begin with, if we are the lone examiners of our heart, a thousand justifications will arise to declare our innocence. . . . At the other end of the spectrum is our tendency for self-flagellation. If left to our own devices, it is so easy for us to take one good look at who we truly are and declare ourselves unredeemable. . . . But with God alongside us, we are protected and comforted. He will never allow us to see more than we are able to handle. (*Prayer*, Foster; p. 29.)

Desire for religious respect or reputation will *immediately* drag us into the rightness of scribes and Pharisees because that desire always focuses entirely upon the visible action, not on the source of action in the heart. The scribes and Pharisees, Jesus pointed out, "do everything they do with the aim of being noticed by others. They enlarge the religious symbols on their clothing. They like to have the most prominent seats at dinners and in the synagogues. They relish loudly respectful greetings in malls and public places, and being called 'Professor' or 'Doctor' " (Matt. 23:5-7). . . . The children of the kingdom, by contrast, are to have none of all this. (*The Divine Conspiracy*, Willard; pp. 188–189.)

People are not noble because they succeed or are applauded by others. Their lives are honorable and worthy of emulation because they are striving for what is good—no matter what the results! God asks us to be involved not because we are called to be successful, but because we are called to be *faithful*. Moreover, this very act of faithfulness, no matter how little the impact appears to be, teaches us lessons in perspective and hope which can only be taught by acting compassionately. (*Everyday Simplicity*, Robert J. Wicks; p. 120.)

Remember once again the words of Jesus. Those who make a show of their prayers, their spirituality, have received their reward already. Spirituality at its finest does not call attention to itself. Spirituality at its finest is focused upon and calls attention to God. . . . Spirituality is to walk freely, faithfully, openly, joyfully as liberated children of the living God—at home in God's creation, unafraid of yesterday, today, or tomorrow. One lives, confident that all of life is cared for, nurtured, and preserved by the God of steadfast love without limit. That is cause for celebration and not somberness. (*A Journey Toward Solitude and Community*, Rueben P. Job; p. 53.)

Reflection Time

Making Our Requests Known
Prayer for Our World, Its People and Leaders
Prayer for the Church and Its Leaders
Prayer for Those in Our Circle of Responsibility
Prayer for Ourselves

Offering of Self to God
What shall I return to the LORD
　　for all his bounty to me?
I will lift up the cup of salvation
　　and call on the name of the LORD,
I will pay my vows to the LORD
　　in the presence of all his people. (Psalm 116:12-14)

Blessing
May the LORD give you increase,
　　both you and your children.
May you be blessed by the LORD,
　　who made heaven and earth. (Psalm 115:14-15)

Week 45

GOD'S FAMILY INCLUDES ALL GOD'S CHILDREN

Becoming Aware of God's Presence

I will sing of your steadfast love, O LORD, forever;
   with my mouth I will proclaim your faithfulness to all generations.
I declare that your steadfast love is established forever;
   your faithfulness is as firm as the heavens. (Psalm 89:1-2)

Inviting God's Intervention

But you, O LORD my Lord,
   act on my behalf for your name's sake;
   because your steadfast love is good, deliver me.
For I am poor and needy,
   and my heart is pierced within me. (Psalm 109:21-22)

Listening for God's Voice

Sunday	**A.** Exodus 12:1-14; Psalm 149; Romans 13:8-14; Matthew 18:15-20
	B. Proverbs 22:1-2, 8-9, 22-23; Psalm 125; James 2:1-10, (11-13), 14-17; Mark 7:24-37
	C. Jeremiah 18:1-11; Psalm 139:1-6, 13-18; Philemon 1-21; Luke 14:25-33
Monday	Acts 13:44-52
Tuesday	Acts 15:1-5
Wednesday	Matthew 15:21-28
Thursday	Romans 2:1-16
Friday	Acts 10:9-16
Saturday	Matthew 12:46-50

Essay

There are many who try to squeeze God into a tiny, tiny image of the God made known in Jesus Christ. And most of those efforts are made to determine who is included in God's family. It happened in Jesus' time, too. But as the Gospels make clear, Jesus would have none of it and continued to teach and witness to a God whose love was without limits and who embraced every human family as God's own. If the Pharisees could make God small enough, then they could choose who was included in God's family. But Jesus denounced their efforts and often stepped over tradition and rules to demonstrate that no one was left outside the circle of God's love. This is the good news we can receive with joy and proclaim with confidence. Who will you welcome into the Kingdom today?

Quotations

The first assumption that I make, therefore, is that God loves me as God loves all people, without qualification. The second is related to it, and it was also a long time coming to me. According to such great early Christian teachers of the first five centuries whom I teach, such as Irenaeus, Athanasius, Anthony, and Gregory of Nyssa, all human beings are created in the image of God. To them, to be in the image of God means that all of us are made for the purpose of knowing and loving God and one another and of being loved in turn, not literally in the same way God knows and loves, but in a way appropriate to human beings. (*In Ordinary Time*, Roberta C. Bondi; p. 25.)

Deep listening is the key to developing respect for others, and yet we rarely take the time to truly listen. Instead of listening we assume that we know what the other person is saying. Rather than attending to what is beneath the words, we busy ourselves, formulating a brilliant response. . . . We so often listen to others, and others to us, in this disrespectful manner that we have come to think of it as normal and appropriate. But if we have ever been truly listened to, we know what a gift that can be. (*A Praying Congregation*, Vennard; p. 10.)

Jesus weeps in the face of all the divisions he sees and touches among his people: the poor, the weak, the sick, the crippled, . . . the oppressed, the so-called sinners, . . . and on the other side the rich, the powerful, the comfortable, the "pure," settled in their secure ways. And Jesus weeps in the face of all the divisions, hatred, and oppression between Romans and Jews, Jews and Samaritans, the pure and the impure. The heart of Christ weeps for unity to draw together into the Kingdom, into one city of love, the weak and the strong, the poor and the comfortable, the powerless and the powerful, the Jews and the Gentiles, that there may be no more competition and rivalry, . . . no more racism or sexism, no more rejection of the weak and the powerless, no more aggression, wars, manufacture of armaments. In the vision of Jesus each one has a place and is called to love and to exercise his or her gifts to build the body of community and to reflect the unity of the Trinity. (*Jesus, the Gift of Love*, Vanier; pp. 91–92.)

What a strange fellowship this is, the God-seekers of every land, lifting their voices in the most disparate ways imaginable to the God of all life. How does it sound from above? Like bedlam, or do the strains blend in strange, ethereal harmony? Does one faith carry the lead, or do the parts share in counterpoint and antiphony where not in full-throated chorus? We cannot know. All we can do is try to listen carefully and with full attention to each voice in turn as it addresses the divine. (*The World's Religions*, Huston Smith; p. 2.)

To follow Jesus is to follow a God made known in Scripture, history, nature, our innermost self, and—most of all—in the life, death, and resurrection of Jesus of Nazareth. To follow Jesus is to follow One who fully trusts in God's goodness, love, and intimate involvement in the affairs of humankind. To follow this Jesus is to desire to be like him in our living and our dying. For some of us, that choice is just too frightening and too demanding; so we follow at a distance or turn away. But deep in the silence of our hearts, we know we do want to follow Jesus. We do know that following Jesus is the best and only way for us to live fully and faithfully. We really do know it is the only way to live a peaceful, joyful, faithful life. . . . and so we pray for grace to be faithful. . . . (*Three Simple Rules*, Rueben P. Job; pp. 25–26.)

Reflection Time

Making Our Requests Known
Prayer for Our World, Its People and Leaders
Prayer for the Church and Its Leaders
Prayer for Those in Our Circle of Responsibility
Prayer for Ourselves

Offering of Self to God
I will pay my vows to the LORD
    in the presence of all his people,
in the courts of the house of the LORD,
    in your midst, O Jerusalem.
Praise the LORD! (Psalm 116:18)

Blessing
The LORD has been mindful of us; he will bless us; . . .
he will bless those who fear the LORD,
    both small and great. (Psalm 115:12a, 13)

Week 46
FORGIVENESS

Becoming Aware of God's Presence
Praise the LORD!
> Happy are those who fear the LORD,
> who greatly delight in his commandments. (Psalm 112:1)

Inviting God's Intervention
Help me, O LORD my God!
> Save me according to your steadfast love.
Let them know that this is your hand;
> you, O LORD, have done it. (Psalm 109:26-27)

Listening for God's Voice

Sunday	*A.* Exodus 14:19-31; Psalm 114; Romans 14:1-12; Matthew 18:21-35
	B. Proverbs 1:20-33; Psalm 19; James 3:1-12; Mark 8:27-38
	C. Jeremiah 4:11-12, 22-28; Psalm 14; 1 Timothy 1:12-17; Luke 15:1-10
Monday	Ephesians 4:22-32
Tuesday	Luke 11:20-25
Wednesday	Matthew 7:1-5
Thursday	Matthew 26:26-30
Friday	1 John 2:12-17
Saturday	Romans 4:1-8

Essay
Forgiveness is a life-and-death matter because forgiveness lies at the very heart of Christian belief and practice. To remove forgiveness from our theology and practice is to tear the heart out of any hope of

faithful Christian discipleship, and it is to drive a stake through the heart of Christian community.

This is the reality we confess every time we pray as Jesus taught us to pray. Forgiveness can never be taken lightly by those who consider their own need of forgiveness. The words of Jesus that we pray bind our need for forgiveness firmly to our willingness to forgive. Forgiveness is not only a preposterous gift; it is unbelievably difficult and costly. That is why we may talk about it easily and practice it with such difficulty. To offer forgiveness to a national enemy today will most likely be branded as unpatriotic and to extend forgiveness to another is often branded as being soft and unrealistic. But the forgiveness Jesus taught and practiced is neither soft nor unpatriotic. But it is extremely costly and laden with a mother load of grace for those who practice it. To follow Jesus and adopt his values as our own is to love our enemies and desire their good even when they inflict pain and suffering on those we love. The words of Jesus from the cross, "Father forgive them; for they do not know what they are doing," become the final demonstration on how to forgive. His words and action make me realize anew the unparalleled importance of forgiveness and my own timid practice that should be a way of life.

Quotations

We forgive someone of a wrong they have done us when we decide that we will not make them suffer for it in any way. This does *not* mean we must prevent suffering that may come to them as a result of the wrong they have done. It does not mean that either when we forgive others or when they or God forgive us. Of course we *may* be of help there too, but it is no part of forgiveness. (*The Divine Conspiracy*, Willard; p. 262.)

When Jesus taught the disciples to pray, he grabbed hold of vertical forgiveness, "O Lord, forgive me, for I have sinned," and nailed it to horizontal forgiveness, ". . . as we forgive those who trespass against us," two interrelated acts of forgiveness, forming a cross. Jesus not only taught about forgiveness. He became forgiveness. He makes forgiveness possible and real. (*The Beautiful Work of Learning to Pray*, Howell; p. 73.)

[The] authority of compassion is the possibility of man to forgive his brother, because forgiveness is only real for him who has discovered the weakness of his friends and the sins of his enemy in his own heart. . . . A fatherless generation looks for brothers who are able to take away their fear and anxiety, who can open the doors of their narrow-mindedness and show them that forgiveness is a possibility which dawns on the horizon of humanity. (*The Wounded Healer*, Nouwen; pp. 41–42.)

The tragedy of our lives is that, while we suffer from the wounds afflicted on us by those who love us, we cannot avoid wounding those we want to love. . . . It is here that we are called to believe deeply in the truth that all fatherhood and all motherhood come from God. Only God is the father and mother who can love us as we need and want to be loved. This belief, when strongly held, can free us not only to forgive our parents, but also to let our children forgive us. (*Here and Now*, Nouwen; pp. 141–142.)

The communion that we have in and with Christ reverberates in the communion we have with one another. A eucharistic life is a communal life through and through and from start to finish. This means that there are no solitary Christians in the world of salvation. There are no do-it-yourself Christians. There are no self-help Christians. There are no Lone Ranger Christians. The moment the adjective intrudes it cancels the noun. Salvation is not a private deal with God. We are bound by the action of God in Christ to the entire creation that "waits with eager longing for the revealing of the children of God" (Rom. 8:19). Any understanding of salvation that separates us from others is false and sooner or later cripples our participation in what God in Christ is doing in history, saving the world. (*Christ Plays In Ten Thousand Places*, Peterson; p. 211.)

Reflection Time

Making Our Requests Known
Prayer for Our World, Its People and Leaders
Prayer for the Church and Its Leaders
Prayer for Those in Our Circle of Responsibility
Prayer for Ourselves

Offering of Self to God
Praise the LORD!
I will give thanks to the LORD with my whole heart,
    in the company of the upright, in the congregation. (Psalm 111:1)

Blessing
For you shall go out in joy,
    and be led back in peace;
the mountains and the hills before you
    shall burst into song,
    and all the trees of the field shall clap their hands. (Isaiah 55:12)

Week 47
WHAT ARE YOU ARGUING ABOUT?

Becoming Aware of God's Presence
Those who love me, I will deliver;
  I will protect those who know my name.
When they call to me, I will answer them;
  I will be with them in trouble,
  I will rescue them and honor them.
With long life I will satisfy them,
  and show them my salvation. (Psalm 91:14-16)

Inviting God's Intervention
If the LORD had not been my help,
  my soul would soon have lived in the land of silence.
When I thought, "My foot is slipping,"
  your steadfast love, O LORD, held me up.
When the cares of my heart are many,
  your consolations cheer my soul. (Psalm 94:17-19)

Listening for God's Voice
Sunday	*A.* Exodus 16:2-15; Psalm 105:1-6, 37-45; Philippians 1:21-30; Matthew 20:1-16
	B. Proverbs 31:10-31; Psalm 1; James 3:13–4:3, 7-8a; Mark 9:30-37
	C. Jeremiah 8:18–9:1; Psalm 79:1-9; 1 Timothy 2:1-7; Luke 16:1-13
Monday	Matthew 18:1-5
Tuesday	Luke 9:46-50
Wednesday	Matthew 23:1-12
Thursday	Luke 14:7-12
Friday	Psalm 145:10-17
Saturday	James 3:13-18

Essay

As soon as they got in the house at Capernaum, Jesus popped the question that stunned the disciples into complete silence, "What were you arguing about on the way?" No wonder they were speechless; they were arguing about who was the greatest and their silence demonstrated that they knew that what they were arguing about was absolutely contrary to what Jesus had been teaching (Mark 9:33-37).

Sometimes I wonder if the arguing in the church would turn to deafening silence if we listened to and heard the voice of Jesus saying to us, "What are you arguing about?" Who is in and who is out, who is great and who is small, who is worthy and who is not, who is loved and who is not—all are questions Jesus settled long ago and yet they are so often the center of our conversations.

When this happened with the twelve, Jesus sat down and called them to him and explained to them once more what it meant to live in the kingdom of God. He explained to them once again what it meant to follow him and to be like him. Rather than arguing, perhaps we should be asking Jesus to make his way plain to us this day and every day.

Quotations

Dear Friend, being the Beloved is the origin and the fulfillment of the life of the Spirit. I say this because, as soon as we catch a glimpse of this truth, we are put on a journey in search of the fullness of that truth and we will not rest until we can rest in that truth. From the moment we claim the truth of being the Beloved, we are faced with the call to become who we are. Becoming the Beloved is the great spiritual journey we have to make. Augustine's words: "My soul is restless until it rests in you, O God," capture well this journey. I know that the fact that I am always searching for God, always struggling to discover the fullness of Love, always yearning for the complete truth, tells me that I have already been given a taste of God, of Love, and of Truth. I can only look for something that I have, to some degree, already found. (*Life of the Beloved*, Nouwen; pp. 37–38.)

Jesus said, "Learn from me, for I am gentle and humble in heart" (Matt. 11:29). In what did the humility of Jesus consist? Low self-esteem, feelings of unworthiness, disappointment with his spiritual progress? Absurd! He was enthralled with his Father. In utter self-forgetfulness, he lived for God. The central theme in his personal life was the growing intimacy with, trust in, and love of his Abba. He lived securely in his Father's acceptance. "As the Father has loved me so have I loved you" (John 15:9), he reassures us. Jesus' inner life was centered in God. His communion with his Abba transformed his vision of reality, enabling him to perceive divine love toward sinners and scalawags. Jesus did not live from himself or for himself but from the graciousness of the Other, who is incomprehensibly caring. He understood his Father's compassionate heart. (*Ruthless Trust*, Manning; p. 125.)

The first thing centering prayer is not is a relaxation exercise. It may bring relaxation, but that is strictly a side effect. It is primarily a relationship, hence, intentionality. It is not a technique, it is prayer. When we say, . . . "Let us pray," we mean, "Let us enter into a relationship with God"; or, "Let us deepen the relationship we have"; or, "Let us exercise our relationship with God." Centering prayer is a method of moving our developing relationship with God to the level of pure faith. Pure faith is faith that is moving beyond the rational level of discursive meditation and particular acts to the intuitive level of our being. (*Open Mind, Open Heart*, Keating; p. 133.)

I've never understood how to walk beside the ogres and monsters of this career-driven culture, so rife with fire-breathing options and man-eating standards. I've never quite figured out how to blow fresh air into buried dreams or pull out maidenly features to win the favor of some boss-king. Sure, I could do practical things, like dust off my résumé and send it to that PR firm. I could revisit an old fantasy for radio and call that producer or venture into a new land altogether as an apprentice to a photographer. I *could*. But the *should* whispering from my shoulder draws gigantic question marks in my soul. And so

the cautions of culture linger long in this place called vocation. . . .
And I ask, what *should* I do to earn a living? Why is living something to be earned anyway? How come *this* road feels so bumpy, so dangerous? So littered with ghosts and daggers, tricks and treasures? Why is it so hard to know what to do with our lives? The question prods me daily. But so far I have not found many answers in the Classifieds section. (*Woman Overboard*, Kadlecek; p. 62.)

Reflection Time

Making Our Requests Known
Prayer for Our World, Its People and Leaders
Prayer for the Church and Its Leaders
Prayer for Those in Our Circle of Responsibility
Prayer for Ourselves

Offering of Self to God
O come, let us worship and bow down,
    let us kneel before the LORD, our Maker!
For he is our God,
    and we are the people of his pasture,
    and the sheep of his hand.

O that today you would listen to his voice! (Psalm 95:6-7)

Blessing
Light dawns for the righteous,
    and joy for the upright in heart.
Rejoice in the LORD, O you righteous,
    and give thanks to his holy name! (Psalm 97:11-12)

Week 48

GOD IS AT WORK IN YOU

Becoming Aware of God's Presence

Praise the LORD!
Praise the LORD from the heavens;
     praise him in the heights!
Praise him, all his angels;
     praise him, all his host! (Psalm 148:1-2)

Inviting God's Intervention

Stretch out your hand from on high;
     set me free and rescue me from the mighty waters . . . (Psalm 144:7a)

Listening for God's Voice

Sunday	**A.** Exodus 17:1-7; Psalm 78:1-4, 12-16; Philippians 2:1-13; Matthew 21:23-32
	B. Esther 7:1-6, 9-10; 9:20-22; Psalm 124; James 5:13-20; Mark 9:38-50
	C. Jeremiah 32:1-3a, 6-15; Psalm 91:1-6, 14-16; 1 Timothy 6:6-19; Luke 16:19-31
Monday	Philippians 2:12-18
Tuesday	Matthew 10:40-42
Wednesday	James 1:2-8
Thursday	James 1:12-18
Friday	2 Corinthians 3:12-18
Saturday	1 Corinthians 3:16-23

Essay

God at work in you is an explosive, earthshaking, and life-changing truth. It is a truth expressed throughout the biblical witness and so very clearly in our Monday reading of Philippians 2:13. At this very moment, whoever and wherever you are, something beyond our full comprehension is taking place within your life and mine. The infinite God of love has chosen to become resident within you and to work within you for pure good. Since God is pure goodness and has no ulterior motives, we can trust, embrace, and cooperate with the divine work going on within us and every child of God.

Once we accept this truth and fully embrace this Divine Presence within us, many other things become clear and possible. We can listen to and follow the guidance of the One who made us, loves us, and is able to lead us in the way of God. We can hear and respond to the Divine call to communion and community with the present and living God. We can hear and respond to the call to faithfulness and service because we are no longer on our own, but the power and the presence of the God at work within us is ready, available, and capable to form, transform, and shape us into the beautiful, faithful, and good persons we were created to become. We can now walk through each day without fear because we remember that we do not walk alone but always with the companionship and help of the One who is now at work within us. Let's remember and remind each other often of this radical and revolutionary truth.

Quotations
Jesus teaches us that prayer is fundamentally a loving listening to God as he continually communicates his love to us at each moment. We pray when we are attentive to the presence of God, when we lift our hearts and minds to God's communicating presence. God does not begin and then cease to enter into this loving self-giving. His Son, Jesus, realized in his prayer that his Father surrounded him at every moment of his earthly existence with his Spirit. He opened himself to receive that "invasion" of his Father's goodness by yielding actively to whatever the Father was asking of him in each moment. Thus, Jesus prayed always in whatever he was engaged in doing. Prayer, for Jesus, was not an activity in which he engaged before he did something else. It was a permanent, ever-increasing state of being

turned inwardly toward the Father at every moment in loving trust and self-surrender. Prayer became synonymous with loving surrender based on a childlike trust. "My son, attend to me, keep your eyes fixed on my advice" (Prv 23:26). (*In Jesus We Trust*, Maloney; pp. 36–37.)

We are like children being taught a job by a loving parent who teaches by allowing us to help with the job. And what is such guidance of a child by a parent worth unless there is an eager, but docile response on the part of the child? The whole value of an interior life depends on this: that no bit of it ever is done alone because we think we know how, but always in response to the gentle guidance and teaching of God. (*The Ways of the Spirit*, Underhill; p. 189.)

Living a forgiven life is more than simply relief that we have been absolved. Forgiveness is living with the abiding sense of what our relationship with God and other people can be, and so forgiveness motivates us, admonishes us, provokes us to enrich our poor relationships. Or as Abraham Lincoln put it to a startled questioner near the end of the Civil War: "Madam, do I not destroy my enemies when I make them my friends?" God has destroyed us as enemies, and made us friends, which pivots us outward to destroy our own enemies by making them our friends. Prayer is friendship. (*The Beautiful Work of Learning to Pray*, Howell; p. 74.)

In each moment we are called to risk and to live in trust by staking everything on God's loving fidelity to us. We cannot fathom how God will be present in each given event. Still we hope and trust in his loving presence. We allow him to possess us totally in each moment. And we can do so only because the Holy Spirit *inspires* us. He breathes into us a trust in God's goodness and perfect holiness. Our hope is in him, even as we look at our own poverty and inability to understand or even cope with the given situation. Like loving children, which really we are, we are at peace with our complete surrender to him. We no longer nervously want to control ourselves, or even God, or other persons around us. A gentle openness to each event and all persons involved becomes an habitual attitude on our part. (*In Jesus We Trust*, Maloney; pp. 87–88.)

We have often seen children take on the qualities of their parents and students begin to reflect in their lives the life and ways of their teachers. To live in an intimate relationship with Christ is to begin to act like Christ, to think like Christ, and to be Christ-like in our living. Life in Christ brings great gifts that so many times are left unclaimed by those of us who start the Christian journey but are quick to turn away from the fullness of life that is offered. Our inheritance of assurance, comfort, peace, and life abundant and eternal is often not incorporated into our daily life. Because it is not, we live anxious, fearful, and incomplete lives, and we begin to wonder what difference our faith really makes. Life in Christ changes all of that as we live in the presence and power of Jesus Christ. (*A Wesleyan Spiritual Reader*, Job; p. 37.)

Reflection Time

Making Our Requests Known
Prayer for Our World, Its People and Leaders
Prayer for the Church and Its Leaders
Prayer for Those in Our Circle of Responsibility
Prayer for Ourselves

Offering of Self to God
Praise the LORD!
Praise the LORD, O my soul!
I will praise the LORD as long as I live;
    I will sing praises to my God all my life long. (Psalm 146:1-2)

Blessing
The LORD will fulfill his purpose for me;
    your steadfast love, O LORD, endures forever.
Do not forsake the work of your hands. (Psalm 138:8)

Week 49

LIVING AS A CHILD OF GOD

Becoming Aware of God's Presence

Listen to me, you that pursue righteousness,
  you that seek the LORD.
Look to the rock from which you were hewn,
  and to the quarry from which you were dug. . . .

Listen to me, my people,
  and give heed to me, my nation;
for a teaching will go out from me,
  and my justice for a light to the peoples. (Isaiah 51:1, 4)

Inviting God's Intervention

Yet, O LORD, you are our Father;
  we are the clay, and you are our potter;
  we are all the work of you hand. (Isaiah 64:8)

Listening for God's Voice

Sunday	***A.*** Exodus 20:1-4, 7-9, 12-20; Psalm 19; Philippians 3:4b-14; Matthew 21:33-46
	B. Job 1:1; 2:1-10; Psalm 26; Hebrews 1:1-4; 2:5-12; Mark 10:2-16
	C. Lamentations 1:1-6; Psalm 137; 2 Timothy 1:1-14; Luke 17:5-10
Monday	Matthew 19:13-15
Tuesday	Matthew 18:1-5
Wednesday	Isaiah 40:6-11
Thursday	John 1:10-18
Friday	Luke 18:15-17
Saturday	Ephesians 4:7-16

Essay

They just didn't get it. Time and time again Jesus demonstrated to the disciples what it means to live as a faithful child of God. And time and time again the ways of the culture and their old habits got the best of them and they found themselves vying for the best seats, the places of power, the recognition of their rank among the twelve, and the willingness to manipulate the system to get what they wanted.

My temptation is to be harsh and judgmental toward the twelve. But then, I stop to think about the world in which they lived and realize that for the most part they had taken a giant leap of faith out of and over the culture of their time to a more faithful way of living. Yes, they stumbled now and then. But for the most part, they kept their eye on and tried to practice what Jesus taught and lived in their presence every day. That is what I am going to try today and every day that God grants to me. It will take a giant leap of faith to get out of and over the expectations and practices of the culture in which we live, but the way of living that Jesus offers is a million to one winner over what our culture offers. Let's help each other practice what Jesus taught and lived.

Quotations

To pray "O almighty, eternal, infinite Abba" not only avoids mere sentimentality; it speaks to what I believe is the most important and urgent requirement of our generation—a new awareness of *transcendence*. Such an awareness in no way diminishes the warmth and tenderness of the label "Abba." To address God in this way is the boldest and simplest expression of the absolute trust that God is good, that he is on our side, "that as tenderly as a father treats his children, so Yahweh treats those who fear him" (Ps. 103:13). The awareness of transcendence restores reverence, wonder, awe, and adoration to the "Abba, I belong to you" prayer. It is the Christian complement to the lapidary statement found in the Hasidic tradition: "Fear without love is an imperfection; love without fear is nothing at all." (*Ruthless Trust*, Manning; pp. 106–107.)

The young man held and blessed by the father is a poor, a very poor, man. He left home with much pride and money, determined to live his own life far away from his father and his community. He returns with nothing: his money, his health, his honor, his self-respect, his reputation . . . everything has been squandered. . . . What happened to the son in the distant country? Aside from all the material and physical consequences, what were the inner consequences of the son's leaving home? The sequence of events is quite predictable. The farther I run away from the place where God dwells, the less I am able to hear the voice that calls me the Beloved, and the less I hear the voice, the more entangled I become in the manipulations and power games of the world. (*The Return of the Prodigal Son*, Nouwen; pp. 45–47.)

Let all our employment be to *know* GOD; the more one *knows* Him, the more one *desires* to know Him. And as *knowledge* is commonly the measure of *love*, the deeper and more extensive our *knowledge* shall be, the greater will be our *love*; and if our love of GOD were great, we should love Him equally in pains and pleasures. (*The Practice of the Presence of God*, Brother Lawrence; p. 58.)

God's goodness is his most beautiful and sweet perfection. It is not one of his many attributes. It is his very essence. He cannot be what he is, the absolute God, without also being goodness by nature. We will see that we come to trust in him in all his works toward us because all such acts flow from his very nature as goodness. We stand in amazement of God's omnipotent power. This knowledge comes to us through our understanding of cause and effect. We understand God's wisdom in ordering all things harmoniously, and this astonishes us unceasingly. But God as good and bountiful is an object of our will that brings forth love and desire. (*In Jesus We Trust*, Maloney; p. 22.)

Reflection Time

Making Our Requests Known

Prayer for Our World, Its People and Leaders
Prayer for the Church and Its Leaders
Prayer for Those in Our Circle of Responsibility
Prayer for Ourselves

Offering of Self to God

I call upon you, O LORD; come quickly to me;
    give ear to my voice when I call to you.
Let my prayer be counted as incense before you,
    and the lifting up of my hands as an evening sacrifice. (Psalm 141: 1-2)

Blessing

He gives power to the faint,
    and strengthens the powerless.
Even youths will faint and be weary,
    and the young will fall exhausted;
but those who wait for the LORD shall renew their strength,
    they shall mount up with wings like eagles,
they shall run and not be weary,
    they shall walk and not faint. (Isaiah 40:29-31)

Week 50

PRIVILEGE AND RESPONSIBILITY OF RICHES

Becoming Aware of God's Presence

Who is like the LORD our God,
  who is seated on high,
who looks far down
  on the heavens and the earth?
He raises the poor from the dust,
  and lifts the needy from the ash heap,
to make them sit with princes,
  with the princes of the people. (Psalm 113:5-8)

Inviting God's Intervention

Then I called on the name of the LORD:
  "O LORD, I pray, save my life!"

Gracious is the LORD and righteous;
  our God is merciful. (Psalm 116:4-5)

Listening for God's Voice

Sunday	*A.* Exodus 32:1-14; Psalm 106:1-6, 19-23; Philippians 4:1-9; Matthew 22:1-14
	B. Job 23:1-9, 16-17; Psalm 22:1-15; Hebrews 4:12-16; Mark 10:17-31
	C. Jeremiah 29:1, 4-7; Psalm 66:1-12; 2 Timothy 2:8-15; Luke 17:11-19
Monday	Luke 18:18-30
Tuesday	Acts 14:21-28
Wednesday	2 Thessalonians 3:6-16
Thursday	2 Peter 3:14-18
Friday	Matthew 19:13-30
Saturday	Matthew 6:19-21

Essay

The thundering crash of collapsing financial markets has been heard around the world, as every nation seems to be shuddering under the burden of rising unemployment and falling income. The recent economic storm is described as the worst since the Great Depression. Savings wiped out, homes foreclosed, jobs lost, families with nowhere to live and nothing to eat. What to do? The biblical record is distinctly clear about the kind of life and lifestyle required if the world is to live in peace and prosperity.

It is interesting that Jesus, who had so much to say about money and riches, does not seem to be very concerned about financial collapse but is very concerned about financial responsibility. His concern was for a way of life that was a barrier against what we now experience. Our theme for the week reminds us that each of us has a part to play in joining all who long to see, experience, and work for a breaking out of God's kingdom all around the world as it is in heaven. What steps will we take today to join that faithful community?

Quotations

Christ plays in the community of people with whom we live, and we want to get in on the play. We see what Christ does in creation and history and we want in on it, firsthand with our families and friends and neighbors. But difficulties arise. Soon or late those of us who follow Jesus find ourselves in the company of men and women who also want to get in on it. It doesn't take us long to realize that many of these fellow volunteers and workers aren't much to our liking, and some of them we actively dislike—a mixed bag of saints and sinners, the saints sometimes harder to put up with than the sinners. Jesus doesn't seem to be very discriminating in the children he lets into his kitchen to help with the cooking. (*Christ Plays in Ten Thousand Places*, Peterson; p. 226.)

"The love of money," we know, "is the root of all evil;" but not the thing itself. The fault does not lie in the money, but in them that use it. It may be used ill: And what may not? But it may likewise be used well: It is full as applicable to the best, as to the worst uses. It is of unspeakable service to all civilized nations, in all the common affairs of life: It is a most compendious instrument of transacting all manner of business, and (if we use it according to Christian wisdom) of doing all manner of good. . . . it is an excellent gift of God, answering the noblest ends. In the hands of his children, it is food for the hungry, drink for the thirsty, raiment for the naked: It gives to the traveller and the stranger where to lay his head. By it we may supply the place of an husband to the widow, and of a father to the fatherless. We may be a defence for the oppressed, a means of health to the sick, of ease to them that are in pain; it may be as eyes to the blind, as feet to the lame; yea, a lifter up from the gates of death! (John Wesley, "Sermon 50, The Use of Money," Vol. 6; p. 126.)

Nearly every time he speaks for any length of time, mostly to tell stories or to suggest to the disciples they've missed the point once again, Jesus finds a way to work in some thoughts on living abundantly. . . . Only he'd never have made the best-seller list, given that his road to riches and security always begins with emptying out—of possessions, of self. . . . Instead of tips on turning the perfect real estate trick, or investing in venture capital, Jesus ignores the crowds to listen to the poor mother on public assistance. When he's approached by the earnest young Fortune 500 CEO, . . . Jesus bluntly—with a compassionate look in his eye—counsels the young man to cash in his stock and give the proceeds away. All proceeds. . . . Give your riches away if you want to live richly. The wealthy young model citizen turns back, disheartened and thoroughly rattled. And if we were in his designer shoes? So would we. (*Why Jesus Makes Me Nervous*, Jordan-Lake; pp. 25–26.)

Whoever has food to eat, and raiment to put on, with something [left] over, is rich. Whoever has the necessaries and conveniences of life for himself and his family, and a little to spare for them that have not, is properly a rich man; unless he is a miser, a lover of money, one that hoards up what he can and ought to give to the poor. For if so, he is a poor man still, though he has millions in the bank; yea, he is the poorest of men . . . (John Wesley, "Sermon 126, On the Danger of Increasing Riches," Vol. 7; p. 356.)

Spiritual formation is primarily what the Spirit does, forming the resurrection life of Christ in us. There is not a whole lot we can do here any more than we can create the cosmos (that was the work of the Spirit in creation). . . . But there is a great deal that the Spirit can do—the resurrection community is the Spirit's work. What we can do, need to do, is be there—accept the leaving and the loss of the physically reassuring touch and companionship. Be there to accept what is sent by the Father in Jesus' name. (*Christ Plays in Ten Thousand Places*, Peterson; p. 237.)

Reflection Time

Making Our Requests Known
Prayer for Our World, Its People and Leaders
Prayer for the Church and Its Leaders
Prayer for Those in Our Circle of Responsibility
Prayer for Ourselves

Offering of Self to God
I give you thanks, O LORD, with my whole heart;
    before the gods I sing your praise;
I bow down toward your holy temple
        and give thanks to your name for your steadfast love and your
            faithfulness;
    for you have exalted your name and your word
    above everything. (Psalm 138:1-2)

Blessing
May the God of love and mercy prosper the work of our hands, minds, and hearts and grant us grace to be responsible stewards of each gift bestowed upon us.

Week 51
TO WHOM DO WE BELONG?

Becoming Aware of God's Presence

Seek the LORD while he may be found,
    call upon him while he is near;
let the wicked forsake their way,
    and the unrighteous their thoughts;
let them return to the LORD, that he may have mercy on them,
    and to our God, for he will abundantly pardon. (Isaiah 55:6-7)

Inviting God's Intervention

Search me, O God, and know my heart;
    test me and know my thoughts.
See if there is any wicked way in me,
    and lead me in the way everlasting. (Psalm 139:23-24)

Listening for God's Voice

Sunday	*A.* Exodus 33:12-23; Psalm 99; 1 Thessalonians 1:1-10; Matthew 22:15-22
	B. Job 38:1-7, (34-41); Psalm 104:1-9, 24, 35c; Hebrews 5:1-10: Mark 10:35-45
	C. Jeremiah 31:27-34; Psalm 119:97-104; 2 Timothy 3:14–4:5; Luke 18:1-8
Monday	Romans 15:14-21
Tuesday	Galatians 6:1-10
Wednesday	Luke 20:20-26
Thursday	Luke 23:1-5
Friday	1 Corinthians 3:1-9
Saturday	John 10:11-18

Essay

They were out to trap Jesus. It still happens today that leaders, religious and other kinds as well, are asked questions to trap them into saying something that will discredit them or make the questioner look superior. Well, it didn't work with Jesus. The question was about paying taxes (Matthew 22:15-22), and Jesus immediately saw through their scheme and said, "Show me the coin used for the tax." When they produced the coin Jesus asked, "Whose head is on this, and whose title?" They answered, "The emperor's." Jesus then said, "Give therefore to the emperor the things that are the emperor's, and give to God the things that are God's."

It is wonderful to belong and there are countless lesser gods hidden in the glitter of our culture with subtle and flagrant invitations seeking our loyalty and allegiance. However, from the very beginning Christians have maintained that we have been made in the image of God and therefore belong ultimately and only to God in Christ. Often this has been a costly choice, sometimes even demanding the life of the one who maintained loyalty to God in Christ above all else. But the decision was always and ultimately right and rewarding. The Heidelberg catechism declares that "We belong—body and soul, in life and in death—not to ourselves, but to our faithful Savior, Jesus Christ." It is the biblical witness of who God is and who we are and to whom we belong. And it is enough to keep us safe, secure, and faithful in this troubled world and bring us safely home to our eternal dwelling. It is hard to think of belonging to anyone else.

Quotations

Before any pragmatic, utilitarian, or altruistic motivations, prayer is born of a desire to be with Jesus. . . . To really love someone implies a natural longing for presence and intimate communion. . . . Trappist monk Basil Pennington . . . writes, "A father is delighted when his little one, leaving off his toys and friends, runs to him and climbs into his arms. . . . Our Centering Prayer is much like that. We settle down in our Father's arms, in his loving hands. Our mind, our thoughts, our imaginations may flit about here and there . . . but essentially we are choosing to remain for this time intimately with our Father, giving ourselves to him, receiving his love and care, letting him enjoy us as he will. It is a very simple prayer. It is very childlike prayer. It is prayer that opens out to us all the delights of the Kingdom." (*A Glimpse of Jesus*, Manning; pp. 83–85.)

In surrendering to another, and ultimately to God in unselfish love, we reach the highest state of communication that leads to communion. In such intimate self-giving communion we expand into a conscious awareness of being one in a mutual sharing of the good with both the lover and the beloved, while at the same time we both discover how beautifully unique and free we are to live in goodness toward the other. (*In Jesus We Trust*, Maloney; p. 15.)

Experiencing God's love means experiencing that one has been unreservedly accepted, approved, and infinitely loved, that one can and should accept oneself and one's neighbour. Salvation is joy in God which expresses itself in joy in and with one's neighbour. (*Jesus the Christ*, Walter Kasper; p. 86.)

Prayer, this universal venture into intimacy with God, so basic and easy to begin but so difficult to sustain. Prayer, this so often suppressed or distracted desire to live a life that is more than skin deep. Prayer, not content to live a merely exterior life of job description, hair color, and complexion. Prayer, a refusal to live as an outsider to my God and my own soul. Prayer, this "best" that is so easily corrupted into the "worst," its rich interior maturity deteriorated into a kitchen midden of pious clichés. Two contrasting characters, a Pharisee and a tax collector, provide the action of the story. But what catches my attention at the outset is what they have in common: they both go to the same church (the temple), they both pray when they get there, and they are both sinners. (*Tell It Slant*, Peterson; pp. 135–136.)

Prayer is not begging God to do something for us that he is reluctant to do, or begging God to do something that he hasn't time for. In prayer we persistently, faithfully, trustingly come before God, submitting ourselves to his sovereignty, confident that he is acting, right now, on our behalf. We are his "chosen ones," and don't forget it. God is, right now—the word is "quickly" . . . working his will in your life and circumstances. So keep praying. Don't quit. (*Tell It Slant*, Peterson; p. 144.)

Reflection Time

Making Our Requests Known
Prayer for Our World, Its People and Leaders
Prayer for the Church and Its Leaders
Prayer for Those in Our Circle of Responsibility
Prayer for Ourselves

Offering of Self to God
I say to the LORD, "You are my God;
  give ear, O LORD, to the voice of my supplications." (Psalm 140:6)

Blessing
Finally, brothers and sisters, . . . agree with one another, live in peace; and the God of love and peace will be with you. (2 Corinthians 13:11)

Week 52
SIMPLE AND COMPLETE

Becoming Aware of God's Presence

When the LORD restored the fortunes of Zion,
    we were like those who dream.
Then our mouth was filled with laughter,
    and our tongue with shouts of joy;
then it was said among the nations,
    "The LORD has done great things for them."
The LORD has done great things for us,
    and we rejoiced. (Psalm 126:1-3)

Inviting God's Intervention

Restore our fortunes, O LORD,
    like the watercourses in the Negeb.
May those who sow in tears
    reap with shouts of joy.
Those who go out weeping,
    bearing the seed for sowing,
shall come home with shouts of joy,
    carrying their sheaves. (Psalm 126:4-6)

Listening for God's Voice

Sunday	*A.* Deuteronomy 34:1-12; Psalm 90:1-6, 13-17; 1 Thessalonians 2:1-8; Matthew 22:34-46
	B. Job 42:1-6, 10-17; Psalm 34:1-8, (19-22); Hebrews 7:23-28; Mark 10:46-52
	C. Joel 2:23-32; Psalm 65; 2 Timothy 4:6-8, 16-18; Luke 18:9-14
Monday	Mark 12:28-34
Tuesday	Deuteronomy 6:4-9

Wednesday	Luke 11:9-13
Thursday	1 Timothy 1:3-7
Friday	Romans 12:9-21
Saturday	Deuteronomy 30:11-14

Essay

It is so very simple and so very complete. We like to make it complex, hard to understand, and easy to avoid. But Jesus had a way of cutting through all the rules and their explanations to reveal the core truth of a faithful life. It was simple, challenging, and profound. His teaching was so clear it was hard to miss the point and so profound that it would take a lifetime of practice to fulfill its challenge. One day Jesus was confronted by some Pharisees about which commandment in the law was the greatest (Matthew 22:36). It could have been an honest question, or just another way to try to make Jesus appear irrelevant or wrong. And once again Jesus not only gives a clear and wise answer, but in doing so he gives a simple and complete blueprint for a life of faithfulness. Love God with all of your being and love your neighbor as you love yourself. I can understand that, remember it, and for all my days I will try to practice this simple and complete way of faithful living.

Quotations

A prayer practice is just that: practice. It is taking time to learn how to listen for God. It is taking time to see the hand of God at work in our lives. We need to take this time because this listening, this seeing are difficult tasks. I once introduced a time of silent prayer at a prayer service by saying, "Let us take some time to listen to God." One woman who was struggling with various concerns said, "I listen and all I hear is the fan on the ceiling." God's voice is often very soft. Prayer practice is the art of setting aside our own individual desires to seek the desire that God has placed on our heart. It is becoming aware of the distractions of our minds and then letting them go, and as we repeat the disciplines over time, we become more skilled at seeing God in all that we do. (*Creating a Life With God*, Wolpert; p. 18.)

We need not take on great tasks or engage in noble causes. What we do in the service of others can be externally insignificant, but, if motivated by love for the One who sacrificed himself for us, "though it be as insignificant as an ant" (Abbé Monchanin), it assumes great power and is worth much in the sight of God. "In the evening of our life," John of the Cross reminds us, "we will be judged not by our works but by our love." With the gift of contemplation comes the responsibility to act in accordance with the magnitude of the gift, for we never receive it exclusively for ourselves but to serve others. (*Why Not Be a Mystic?* Frank X. Tuoti; p. 157.)

The question Jesus asked of Peter in John 21:15ff, "Do you love me?" reveals a great deal about the essentials of our relationship with God. Three times Jesus asked, "Do you love me?" and three times Peter answered in the affirmative. Staying in love with God was the primary issue of a faithful life then, and it is today. For from such a life of love for God will flow the goodness and love of God to the world. It can be no other way. One who is deeply in love will be constantly formed and transformed by that relationship. And such a transformed life will be a natural channel of God's goodness, power, and presence in the world. (*Three Simple Rules*, Job; pp. 57–58.)

No really good work of any kind is ever really done unless it is done in love, joy, and peace, so that unless these characteristics are established in our souls, and nourished by prayer and adoration, it is not likely that they will ever fully come to us in the pressure and difficulties of active life. . . . A modern saint has said, with the directness and simplicity of the saints, that the bread of life seldom has any butter on it. And this is so just because it is life and not a lovely dream or a heavenly vision: a life which is full of tension and of difficulty, and full of opportunities for heroic choice and for sacrifice in spiritual as well as in material things. . . . Love, work, and suffer: the work must be done in joy, and the suffering must be accepted in peace, and this cannot and will not happen unless both are rooted and grounded in love—the one absolute essential of the inner life and the one guarantee of the growth of the soul towards God. (*The Ways of the Spirit*, Underhill; p. 60.)

Therefore, each time Jesus raised the question, "Do you love me?" he also declared how Peter and the world would know if he was obedient to God. Holy living will not be discovered, achieved, continued, and sustained without staying in love with God. And while staying in love with God involves prayer, worship, study, and the Lord's Supper, it also involves feeding the lambs, tending the sheep, and providing for the needs of others (John 21:15-16). Feeding the lambs and tending the sheep are the signs of love that we exchange with God. And they are signs of love that the world can understand. (*Three Simple Rules*, Job; p. 58.)

Reflection Time

Making Our Requests Known
Prayer for Our World, Its People and Leaders
Prayer for the Church and Its Leaders
Prayer for Those in Our Circle of Responsibility
Prayer for Ourselves

Offering of Self to God
I wait for the LORD, my soul waits,
 and in his word I hope;
my soul waits for the Lord
 more than those who watch for the morning,
 more than those who watch for the morning. (Psalm 130:5-6)

Blessing
May the LORD, maker of heaven and earth,
 bless you . . . (Psalm 134:3)

Week 53

ALL THINGS ARE POSSIBLE WITH GOD

Becoming Aware of God's Presence

Come, bless the LORD, all you servants of the LORD,
　who stand by night in the house of the LORD!
Lift up your hands to the holy place,
　and bless the LORD. (Psalm 134:1-2)

Inviting God's Intervention

Do good, O LORD, to those who are good,
　and to those who are upright in their hearts. (Psalm 125:4)

Listening for God's Voice

Sunday	*A.* Joshua 3:7-17; Psalm 107:1-7, 33-37; 1 Thessalonians 2:9-13; Matthew 23:1-12
	B. Ruth 1:1-18; Psalm 146; Hebrews 9:11-14; Mark 12:28-34
	C. Habakkuk 1:1-4; 2:1-4; Psalm 119:137-144; 2 Thessalonians 1:1-4, 11-12; Luke 19:1-10
Monday	Luke 5:27-32
Tuesday	2 Corinthians 7:2-12
Wednesday	1 Samuel 12:1-5
Thursday	1 Timothy 1:12-17
Friday	Ezekiel 34:11-16
Saturday	Mark 2:13-17

Essay

It is such a mess that it seems hopeless! We say that about our world, our current global economic situation, the life of a wounded and lost soul, and sometimes even we say it deep in the quiet places of our hearts about ourselves. But when we do we miss the point of much of what Jesus taught. The story of Zacchaeus in Luke 19 is an illustration of God doing the impossible. First of all, Jesus breaks all the cultural and religious barriers by treating a hated tax collector with respect and dignity and then invites himself to dinner at the tax collector's home. A shocking transformation of cultural and religious patterns that seemed unchangeable. And then Jesus heard Zacchaeus declare he would give half his accumulated wealth to the poor. And further, that if there were any fraudulent activity he would repay the amount taken four times over. Here we have a perfect example of God doing what is impossible for mere mortals alone as this rich tax collector, lost and alienated, is "saved" and welcomed home to the kingdom of God (Luke 19:9-10; Matthew 19:23-26). What is on your horizon this week that seems impossible to mere mortals? Why not let it be the focus of your prayers as you ask God to intervene? Perhaps we could all take a lesson from the persistence of the widow who would not relent in her fervent quest for justice until her request was fulfilled (Luke 18:1-8).

Quotations

Churches are notoriously lax about ordering background checks to identify people with criminal records and installing security systems to screen out people who might use the church as a cover for evil. The consequence is that churches collect a lot of undesirable people, men and women who end up being an embarrassment to the company of people who are honestly trying to worship a holy God, to serve the world in acts of love and justice, repentance and forgiveness, and to follow Jesus every day into their homes and workplaces in sacrificial obedience. If the church had run security checks on the Pharisee and the tax man, neither would have gotten through the door. (*Tell It Slant*, Peterson; p. 137.)

I remember the first day I came home. There were four beautiful women walking out onto the porch to say hello. I looked at the gated yard and had a strange feeling that it seemed familiar. I realized that I had lost my way long ago, and coming into this place gave me an almost forgotten sense of peace. When I walked in, there were plants everywhere; and I was crying because of the nice furniture. I loved the soft bed that felt completely different than the prison mattress I had just left. When I went into the kitchen, I rejoiced at the pots and pans, because I remembered the glass jars and spoons I had left on the sidewalk. This was the home I'd almost forgotten about. Thank you, God, for leading me home. (*Find Your Way Home*, the Women of Magdalene with Stevens; p. 104.)

The story of Jesus is recalled once again to empower conversion from greed and disrespect which lead people to rape the earth for profit. Jesus' vision of the reign of God includes wholeness and *shalom* for all creatures, even the least important in the present hierarchy of values, the nonhuman. God's peace links all creatures in a community of life and stands against exploitation even of the least powerful. In the new heaven and the new earth, every created thing will have its own integrity in relationships of mutuality and interdependence. For those who follow Jesus, not self-interest but respect for all of God's creatures is what should hold sway. (*Consider Jesus*, Johnson; p. 140.)

In the end, it really doesn't matter whether I am in darkness or light, for God is everywhere. In the darkness, as the world around me dims, however, I can "see" God more clearly. In the darkness, God dazzles me, an experience shared by Henry Vaughan in his poem "The Night." "There is in God (some say) / A deep, but dazzling darkness." Pray that all of us experience that night, in that deep but dazzling darkness, where we might be in God and where we might live invisible and dim. (*Treasures of Darkness*, Soughers; p. 96.)

Reflection Time

Making Our Requests Known
Prayer for Our World, Its People and Leaders
Prayer for the Church and Its Leaders

Prayer for Those in Our Circle of Responsibility
Prayer for Ourselves

Offering of Self to God

Let me hear your steadfast love in the morning,
  for in you I put my trust.
Teach me the way I should go,
  for to you I lift up my soul. (Psalm 143:8)

Blessing

Happy is everyone who fears the LORD,
  who walks in his ways.
You shall eat the fruit of the labor of your hands;
  you shall be happy, and it shall go well with you. (Psalm 128:1-2)

Week 54

CHILDREN OF THE RESURRECTION

Becoming Aware of God's Presence
Satisfy us in the morning with your steadfast love,
    so that we may rejoice and be glad all our days. (Psalm 90:14)

Inviting God's Intervention
Give ear to my words, O LORD;
    give heed to my sighing.
Listen to the sound of my cry,
    my King and my God,
    for to you I pray.
O LORD, in the morning you hear my voice;
    in the morning I plead my case to you, and watch. (Psalm 5:1-3)

Listening for God's Voice

Sunday	*A.* Joshua 24:1-3a, 14-25; Psalm 78:1-7; 1 Thessalonians 4:13-18; Matthew 25:1-13
	B. Ruth 3:1-5; 4:13-17; Psalm 127; Hebrews 9:24-28; Mark 12:38-44
	C. Haggai 1:15b–2:9; Psalm 98; 2 Thessalonians 2:1-5,13-17; Luke 20:27-38
Monday	Matthew 22:23-33
Tuesday	Mark 12:18-27
Wednesday	1 Corinthians 15:12-28
Thursday	Revelation 7:9-12
Friday	Romans 14:1-9
Saturday	Hebrews 11:13-16

Essay
After a more than a three-year struggle with brain cancer, my brother's primary care physician told him that the disease had outpaced all

treatment options including radiation and chemotherapy. The illness was terminal. My brother, never being slow to respond, replied, "I know I am terminal. So are you. We are all dying. But how long do I have to live?" This was a wonderful and critical moment in my brother's preparation for his own death (Adapted from *Living Fully, Dying Well*; p. 57). Birth and death are very natural and certain parts of all living things. But our culture is in such denial of death that even the church has been far too silent about this our final act of living in this world.

It was not that different in the time of Jesus. Some Sadducees who did not believe in resurrection tried to trap Jesus with a question about heaven and how family relationships would be determined after death in this world. Jesus responded by saying, "Indeed they cannot die anymore, because they are like angels and are children of God, being children of the resurrection" (Luke 20:36). Relationships in heaven are different, but no less real than relationships on earth.

Sometimes we forget who we are. When we face difficult times we forget that Jesus called us children of the resurrection. When we are gliding along in good times and all seems to be so easy, we forget who we are, children of the resurrection. In other words, Jesus reminds us in easy to understand language that we are not limited to our days on earth. Life is indeed eternal, and the natural cycle of birth and death does not set the limits of our existence or our life with God. Yes, we are all terminal in this world, but not in our relationship to God or life in the world to come.

Quotations
From the beginning the Christian proclamation about Jesus Christ, crucified and risen, was possessed of a universal thrust. In short order early missionaries moved outward from Palestine in an effort to reach the whole world. The good news of God's drawing near in liberating compassion to persons dispossessed by sin was too good to be restricted to any one group. The resurrection of Jesus signaled a living future not only for Jewish believers but for the whole human race. Late in the first century this insight was made explicit by one Christian letter writer:

God our Savior "desires all people to be saved and to come to the knowledge of the truth" (1 Tim 2:5). (*Consider Jesus*, Johnson; p. 130.)

Jesus prayed. When we go to language school with Jesus, we pray. But we are not left to figure all this out on our own. We have a primer, these set Jesus prayers. If we are shy, unsure of ourselves, we can pray them with the confidence that we are praying after the manner of the Master. We keep company with Jesus and gradually get the hang of what he is doing and how he is doing it. (*Tell It Slant*, Peterson; p. 165.)

"It was still dark," John says, when Mary headed to the tomb. And what she found there—better yet, what she *didn't* find there!—simply blew her away. "The stone had been removed," John says (20:1). The grave was empty! The body was gone! There was nothing there but the linen cloths that had wrapped up the broken, bloody, lifeless corpse of Jesus. . . . It was still dark when Mary came to the tomb that morning. And there is still more than enough darkness in this world for all of us. But in the darkest place on earth, Mary found the light that shines in the darkness, and the darkness will never be able to overcome it. In the darkness, she met the Risen Christ; and we can meet him there too. (*Strength for the Broken Places*, Harnish; pp. 130–131, 135.)

The poetry in the heart of a person who has been converted and has become a child of God allows him or her to see much more of God in each event [in life] than most others do. God saturates this "now" moment with his personal presence. . . . This makes everything everywhere a sacred place for God to surprise us with his love, which can never be limited to any special place or time or circumstance. (*In Jesus We Trust*, Maloney; p. 134.)

Perhaps you have been to a place where people have prayed for many years such that you can feel the spiritual power there. This feeling is real, not just a hokey idea. When God's presence is invited by the act of someone praying, God shows up. Thus the prayer of the leader acts to invite God into the midst of the community, and this invitation produces results even if the results are not completely clear. (*Leading a Life With God*, Wolpert; p. 60.)

If any of you are around when I have to meet my day, I don't want a long funeral. And if you get somebody to deliver the eulogy, tell them not to talk too long. . . . I'd like somebody to mention that day, that Martin Luther King, Jr., tried to give his life serving others. I'd like for somebody to say that day, that Martin Luther King, Jr., tried to love somebody. I want you to say that day, that I tried to be right on the war question. I want you to be able to say that day, that I did try to feed the hungry. And I want you to be able to say that day, that I did try, in my life, to clothe those who were naked. I want you to say, on that day, that I did try, in my life, to visit those who were in prison. I want you to say that I tried to love and serve humanity. Yes, if you want to say that I was a drum major, say that I was a drum major for justice; say that I was a drum major for peace; I was a drum major for righteousness. And all of the other shallow things will not matter. I won't have any money to leave behind. I won't have the fine and luxurious things of life to leave behind. But I just want to leave a committed life behind. (*A Testament of Hope*, King; p. 267.)

Reflection Time

Making Our Requests Known
Prayer for Our World, Its People and Leaders
Prayer for the Church and Its Leaders
Prayer for Those in Our Circle of Responsibility
Prayer for Ourselves

Offering of Self to God
I cry to you, O LORD;
> I say, "you are my refuge,
> my portion in the land of the living." (Psalm 142:5)

Blessing
May the God of steadfastness and encouragement grant you to live in harmony with one another, in accordance with Christ Jesus, so that together you may with one voice glorify the God and Father of our Lord Jesus Christ. (Romans 15:5-6)

Week 55
A GOOD INVESTMENT

Becoming Aware of God's Presence
God is our refuge and strength,
    a very present help in trouble.
Therefore we will not fear . . . (Psalm 46:1-2a)

Inviting God's Intervention
Answer me, O LORD, for your steadfast love is good;
    according to your abundant mercy, turn to me. (Psalm 69:16)

Listening for God's Voice
Sunday	*A.* Judges 4:1-7; Psalm 123; 1 Thessalonians 5:1-11; Matthew 25:14-30
	B. 1 Samuel 1:4-20; 1 Samuel 2:1-10; Hebrews 10:11-14, (15-18), 19-25; Mark 13:1-8
	C. Isaiah 65:17-25; Isaiah 12; 2 Thessalonians 3:6-13; Luke 21:5-19
Monday	Matthew 24:45-51
Tuesday	Luke 22:28-30
Wednesday	Luke 12:35-40
Thursday	Luke 12:41-48
Friday	2 Timothy 2:1-13
Saturday	Luke 8:16-21

Essay
The story of the talents that Jesus told in Matthew 25:14-30 tells us about the value of a good investment. God gives us the gift of life and every day we have the privilege of investing it wisely. Most of us would like to invest our lives in something good that yields a better world and personal fulfillment and satisfaction for our investment.

To do so takes careful planning and diligent management lest we invest our time, energy, and very lives in ways that diminish the world and ourselves.

We know we cannot determine the measure of the talents God gives to us and we cannot determine the circumstances that are thrust upon us and provide the "market" climate in which we are called to invest our lives. But we do know that God promises to not only provide the "talents" to be invested but also the guidance and companionship that will permit us to invest our lives wisely and well. And when we follow the Spirit's guidance we will be amazed at all those one hundred percent returns that we experience.

Quotations

Three Old Testament themes point to the fullness and the richness of *shalom* as the possibility for which we were created. The first is the theme of creation in the image of God. The Bible affirms the unique and precious quality of every person as a child of God. It also affirms the responsibility of each person. To be created in the image of God is a gift that brings with it the responsibility to care for God's creation (Genesis 1:28). . . . A second important theme from creation theology is the goodness of the creation. At the end of the sixth day, God looked at all that had been made and saw that it was *very* good (Genesis 1:31). The intention of creation was for *shalom* to be experienced by all, for all to know the goodness of creation. . . . A third theme of *shalom* is this: in creation we are all related. Human beings are not self-sufficient. We need relationship to God, to others, and to nature. Jesus, when asked to sum up the Law, sums it up not simply in terms of love of God but love of neighbor as well. . . . We are not only created as stewards of God to experience the goodness of creation, but we are created to be in community with all creation. *Shalom* only finds its fulfillment when we find that interrelatedness. (From "Shalom: Toward a Vision of Human Wholeness," Bruce C. Birch, in *Living Simply*; pp. 80–81.)

I remember when I surrendered myself. It was the biggest turnaround of my life. I got up one morning in the community and took my wig off. I took it off because I needed to be myself. I was ready to stop hiding and ready to start growing. I was ready to work with others and make some changes and see the real me. I wanted to be the person who has dreams and goals and lives them out. I wanted others to see me. I decided that day that I was beautiful even with my scars and messed-up teeth. I knew that God had new plans for me and because of his belief in me that nothing could hurt me. (*Find Your Way Home*, the Women of Magdalene with Stevens; p. 73.)

I suspect that there is more than one thing that we share with God. We certainly are able to love, and in that we reveal something of the God who is love (1 John 4:8). We think and we reason, and in that we share something with God who orders all things. But we also create, a direct connection with God whom we call Creator. Out of the darkness, God's Word created. Among the things God created in this burst of creative energy were human beings, who could continue God's creation. We are each called to create. Some of us create by way of art or music or dance but all of us are called to create our lives out of the raw material that God has given us. We are called to create in honor of and as a reflection of our Creator, and perhaps it is in such creation that we most clearly reflect God's image and likeness. We, too, are called to allow our spirit to sweep over the waters of our darkness, so that we, with the Spirit, may cry, "Let there be light." (*Treasures of Darkness*, Soughers; pp. 14–15.)

Where the Wesleyan movement is vital and actively engaged in mission today, we will find these same great streams of theology. We will find a deep and growing relationship to God that is nurtured by careful attention to and practice of the disciplines of the spiritual life. And out of this life of prayer and devotion flows a determined and unyielding commitment to God's people and their needs. . . . Wesleyans at their best, . . . hold together these three theological strands into one mighty stream of faith and works. When and where, by God's grace, we are able to weave these three strands together, there the Body of Christ is visible and active in the world. There people will see God at work, experience God's love, and find their love for God and neighbor awakened and strengthened. God's love and ours—a trustworthy pathway to faithful discipleship. (*A Wesleyan Spiritual Reader*, Job; p. 202.)

Jesus' inviting us to drink the cup without offering the reward we expect is the great challenge of the spiritual life. It breaks through all human calculations and expectations. It defies all our wishes to be sure in advance. It turns our hope for a predictable future upside down and pulls down our self-invented safety devices. It asks for the most radical trust in God, the same trust that made Jesus drink the cup to the bottom. (*Can You Drink the Cup?* Nouwen; pp. 118–119.)

Reflection Time

Making Our Requests Known
Prayer for Our World, Its People and Leaders
Prayer for the Church and Its Leaders
Prayer for Those in Our Circle of Responsibility
Prayer for Ourselves

Offering of Self to God
O Lord, open my lips,
    and my mouth will declare your praise. (Psalm 51:15)

Blessing
Steadfast love and faithfulness will meet;
    righteousness and peace will kiss each other.
Faithfulness will spring up from the ground,
    and righteousness will look down from the sky.
The LORD will give what is good,
    and our land will yield its increase. (Psalm 85:10-12)

Week 56

COMPLETE AT LAST

Becoming Aware of God's Presence

To you, O LORD, I lift up my soul. . . .
Do not let those who wait for you be put to shame. . . .
Make me to know your ways, O LORD;
    teach me your paths. (Psalm 25:1, 3a, 4)

Inviting God's Intervention

When they had prayed, the place in which they were gathered together was shaken; and they were all filled with the Holy Spirit and spoke the word of God with boldness. (Acts 4:31)

Listening for God's Voice

Sunday	**A.** Ezekiel 34:11-16, 20-24; Psalm 100; Ephesians 1:15-23; Matthew 25:31-46
	B. 2 Samuel 23:1-7; Psalm 132:1-12, (13-18); Revelation 1:4b-8; John 18:33-37
	C. Jeremiah 23:1-6; Luke 1:68-79; Colossians 1:11-20; Luke 23:33-43
Monday	Joel 3:1-2a, 9-17
Tuesday	1 Peter 1:1-12
Wednesday	1 Peter 2:1-10
Thursday	1 Peter 2:11-25
Friday	Matthew 20:17-28
Saturday	Matthew 20:29-34

Essay

Most of us find great satisfaction in a task successfully completed. Seeing a lawn freshly mowed and trimmed, clothes coming from the laundry room fresh and clean, a project completed at work, all bring immediate and long-term rewards. I remember how good it felt as a young farmer to have crops harvested and ample food supply prepared to provide for our livestock until the spring rains and new food would be available. It was a long time until spring, but I knew everything was complete to weather the storms of winter and move into the life-giving days of spring.

This final week of the Christian Year marks God's victory over all that stands in the way of the complete fulfillment of God's will and the full coming of God's kingdom on earth as it is in heaven. Yes, we may still experience the storms of life, but we know that the ultimate victory has been achieved and we move steadily toward that time when the kingdom of God will be complete.

Quotations

A renewed Christian spirituality will be a spirituality which looks to the faith of the Apostolic Church as exhibited in the New Testament: the faith in God who brings unity to the human race, and who has wrought salvation and reconciliation through Christ; a God of light and love; a God whose spirit brings freedom; a God who nourishes and builds up the body of Christ. In the New Testament, as in the Old, it will seek to deepen knowledge of the living and true God. (*The Eye of the Storm*, Leech; p. 218.)

Wisdom teaches that the goal of our lives is to live with God forever. We're pilgrims passing through, and Jesus counsels us to count how few days we have and thus gain wisdom of the heart. When I accept in the depth of my being that the ultimate accomplishment of my life is *me*—the person I've become and who other persons are because of me—then living in the wisdom of accepted tenderness is not a technique, not a craft, not a Carnegian ploy of how to win friends and influence people, but a way of life, a distinctive and engaged presence to God. . . . (*The Wisdom of Tenderness*, Manning; pp. 2–3.)

In reality time is not and never can be sundered from God, the 'present age' from the 'age to come.' Because of this the 'age to come' and its realities must be thought of, not as non-existent or as coming into existence in the future, but as actualities that by grace we can experience here and now. To indicate this, the Greek phrase for these realities . . . is often translated as 'the blessings held in store.' (*The Philokalia*, Vol. 4, St. Nikodimos of the Holy Mountain and St. Makarios of Corinth; p. 427.)

I am a creature of a day, passing through life as an arrow through the air. I am a spirit come from God, and returning to God: Just hovering over the great gulf; till, a few moments hence, I am no more seen; I drop into an unchangeable eternity! I want to know one thing,—the way to heaven; how to land safe on that happy shore. God himself has condescended to teach the way: For this very end he came from heaven. He hath written it down in a book. O give me that book! At any price, give me the book of God! (John Wesley, "Preface," Vol. 5; p. 3.)

There is no one right way to pray. The more we pray and the more we learn about the way others pray, the more sure we become about this. Different approaches abound to provide room for each of us to explore, improvise, and find his or her own way in prayer. They support us as we begin to take hold of the astounding truth that God loves us in the flesh, that our reality is reality. . . . The many different kinds of holy men and women, the lovers of God, each so different in temperament and psychological type, embolden us to believe that each of us can find our own way. (*Primary Speech*, Ulanov; p. 115.)

Reflection Time

Making Our Requests Known
Prayer for Our World, Its People and Leaders
Prayer for the Church and Its Leaders
Prayer for Those in Our Circle of Responsibility
Prayer for Ourselves

Offering of Self to God

I give to you all that I am on this day, and invite your constant presence in my life to guide, direct, use, and sustain as you will.

Blessing

Be strong and courageous; do not be frightened or dismayed, for the LORD your God is with you wherever you go. (Joshua 1:9)

BIBLIOGRAPHY

Barron, Robert. *The Strangest Way: Walking the Christian Path*. Maryknoll, New York: Orbis Books, 2002.

Bass, Dorothy C., ed. *Practicing Our Faith*. San Francisco: Jossey-Bass, 1997.

Benedict, Jr., Daniel T. *Patterned by Grace*. Nashville: Upper Room Books, 2007.

Birch, Bruce C. "Shalom: Toward a Vision of Human Wholeness," *Living Simply*. New York: Seabury Press, 1981.

Blumhardt, Christoph Friedrich. "Action in Waiting," *Watch for the Light*. Maryknoll, New York: Plough Publishing, 2001.

Bondi, Roberta C. *In Ordinary Time*. Nashville: Abingdon Press, 1996.

———. *Memories of God*. Nashville: Abingdon Press, 1995.

Borg, Marcus J. *The Heart of Christianity: Rediscovering a Life of Faith*. New York: HarperSanFrancisco, 2003.

Brame, Grace Adolphsen. *Faith, the Yes of the Heart*. Minneapolis, Minnesota: Augsburg Fortress, 1999.

Brother Lawrence. *The Practice of the Presence of God*. Radford, Virginia: Wilder, 2008.

Brueggemann, Walter, Sharon Parks, and Thomas H. Groome. *To Act Justly, Love Tenderly, Walk Humbly*. Mahwah, New Jersey: Paulist Press, 1986.

Casey, Michael. *Toward God: The Ancient Wisdom of Western Prayer*. Liguori, Missouri: Liguori/Triumph, 1996.

Chittister, Joan. *Illuminated Life*. Maryknoll, New York: Orbis Books, 2000.

Day, Albert Edward. *An Autobiography of Prayer*. New York: Harper & Brothers, 1952.

Fénelon, François. *The Royal Way of the Cross*, ed. Hal M. Helms. Brewster, Massachusetts: Paraclete Press, 1982.

Foster, Richard J. *Prayer: Finding the Heart's True Home*. New York: HarperCollins, 1992.

Funk, Mary Margaret. *Tools Matter for Practicing the Spiritual Life*. New York: Continuum, 2001.

Greer, Ronald J. *If You Know Who You Are You'll Know What to Do*. Nashville: Abingdon Press, 2009.

Gula, S. S., Richard M. *To Walk Together Again*. Ramsey, New Jersey: Paulist Press, 1984.

Hahn, Celia Allison. *Growing in Authority, Relinquishing Control*. Herndon, Virginia: Alban Institute, 1994.

Harnish, James A. *Strength for the Broken Places*. Nashville: Abingdon Press, 2009.

Hauser, S. J., Richard J. *Moving in the Spirit*. Mahwah, New Jersey: Paulist Press, 1986.

Hinson, E. Glenn. *Spiritual Preparation for Christian Leadership*. Nashville: Upper Room Books, 1999.

Howell, James C. *The Beautiful Work of Learning to Pray*. Nashville: Abingdon Press, 2003.

———. *The Kiss of God*. Nashville: Abingdon Press, 2004.

Job, Rueben P. *A Guide to Spiritual Discernment*. Nashville: Upper Room Books, 1996.

———. *A Journey Toward Solitude and Community*. Nashville: Upper Room Books, 1982.

———. *Living Fully, Dying Well*. Nashville: Abingdon Press, 2006.

———. *Three Simple Rules*. Nashville: Abingdon Press, 2007.

———. *A Wesleyan Spiritual Reader*. Nashville: Abingdon Press, 1998. Used by permission.

Johnson, Elizabeth A. *Consider Jesus*. New York: Crossroad, 1990.

Johnson, Luke Timothy. *The Creed*. New York: Doubleday, 2003.

Jordan-Lake, Joy. *Why Jesus Makes Me Nervous*. Brewster, Massachusetts: Paraclete Press, 2007.

Julian, C. S. F., Helen. *The Road to Emmaus*. Nashville: Upper Room Books, 2006.

Kadlecek, Jo. *Woman Overboard*. Nashville: Fresh Air Books, 2009.

Kasper, Walter. *Jesus the Christ*. Mahwah, New Jersey: Paulist Press, 1976.

Keating, Thomas. *Invitation to Love*. Rockport, Massachusetts: Element, 1992.

———. *Open Mind, Open Heart: The Contemplative Dimension of the Gospel*. New York: Continuum, 1992.

Kelly, O. S. F., Carole Marie. *Symbols of Inner Truth*. Mahwah, New Jersey: Paulist Press, 1988.

À Kempis, Thomas. *The Imitation of Christ*, contemporary text by William C. Creasy. Notre Dame, Indiana: Ave Maria Press, 2004.

King, Jr., Martin Luther. *A Testament of Hope*, ed. James M. Washington. New York: HarperSanFrancisco, 1986.

Kinnaman, David and Gabe Lyons. *Unchristian*. Grand Rapids, Michigan: Baker Books, 2007.

Kornfield, Jack. *A Path With Heart*. New York: Bantam Books, 1993.

Langford, Thomas A. *Practical Divinity*, Vol. 1. Nashville: Abingdon Press, 1998. Used by permission.

Leech, Kenneth. *The Eye of the Storm*. London: Darton, Longman, and Todd, 1992.

Maloney, S. J., George A. *In Jesus We Trust*. Notre Dame, Indiana: Ave Maria Press, 1990.

Manning, Brennan. *Abba's Child*. Colorado Springs: NavPress, 2002.

———. *A Glimpse of Jesus: The Stranger to Self-Hatred*. New York: HarperCollins, 2003.

———. *Ruthless Trust: The Ragamuffin's Path to God*. New York: HarperSanFrancisco, 2000.

———. *The Wisdom of Tenderness*. New York: HarperCollins, 2002.

Moltmann, Jürgen. "The Disarming Child," *Watch for the Light*. Maryknoll, New York: Plough Publishing, 2001.

Mother Teresa. *A Simple Path*. New York: Ballantine, 1995.

Mouw, Richard J. *Consulting the Faithful*. Grand Rapids, Michigan: Wm. B. Eerdmans, 1994.

Muto, Susan. *Late Have I Loved Thee*. New York: Crossroad, 1995.

Niederauer, George H. *Precious as Silver: Imagining Your Life With God*. Notre Dame, Indiana: Ave Maria Press, 2004.

Norris, Kathleen. *Amazing Grace*. New York: Riverhead Books, 1998.

Nouwen, Henri J. M. *Can You Drink the Cup?* Notre Dame, Indiana: Ave Maria Press, 2006.

———. *Here and Now*. New York: Crossroad, 1994.

———. *Life of the Beloved*. New York: Crossroad, 1992.

———. *The Return of the Prodigal Son*. New York: Doubleday, 1992.

———. *Sabbatical Journey*. New York: Crossroad, 1998.

————. *The Wounded Healer*. New York: Image, 1972.

Oliva, S. J., Max. *Free to Pray, Free to Love*. Notre Dame, Indiana: Ave Maria Press, 1994.

Peterson, Eugene H. *Christ Plays in Ten Thousand Places*. Grand Rapids, Michigan: Wm. B. Eerdmans, 2005)

————. *Tell It Slant*. Grand Rapids, Michigan: Wm. B. Eerdmans, 2008.

Rohr, Richard. *Everything Belongs*. New York: Crossroad, 1999.

Rupp, Joyce. *The Cup of Our Life*. Notre Dame, Indiana: Ave Maria Press, 1997.

Saint Nikodimos of the Holy Mountain and Saint Makarios of Corinth. *The Philokalia*, Vol. 2., trans. and ed. G. E. H. Palmer, Philip Sherrard, Kallistos Ware. Boston: Faber and Faber, 1981.

————. *The Philokalia*, Vol. 4., trans. and ed. G. E. H. Palmer, Philip Sherrard, Kallistos Ware. Boston: Faber and Faber, 1995.

Shannon, William H. *Seeds of Peace*. New York: Crossroad, 1996.

Shawchuck, Norman and Rueben P. Job. *A Guide to Prayer for All Who Seek God*. Nashville: Upper Room Books, 2006.

Smith, Huston. *The Soul of Christianity*. New York: HarperSanFrancisco, 2005.

————. *The World's Religions*. New York: HarperCollins, 1991.

Soughers, Tara. *Treasures of Darkness*. Nashville: Abingdon Press, 2009. Used by permission.

Steere, Douglas V. *Dimensions of Prayer*. New York: Women's Division, The General Board of Global Ministries, The United Methodist Church, 1962. (An updated edition of this book was published by Upper Room Books in 1997.)

Stevens, Becca. *Hither and Yon*. Nashville: Dimensions for Living, 2007. Used by permission.

Taylor, Barbara Brown. *An Altar in the World*. New York: HarperOne, 2009.

Thompson, Marjorie J. *Family: The Forming Center*. Nashville: Upper Room Books, 1989.

Tuoti, Frank X. *Why Not Be a Mystic?* New York: Crossroad, 1995.

Ulanov, Ann and Barry. *Primary Speech: A Psychology of Prayer*. Atlanta: John Knox Press, 1982.

Underhill, Evelyn. *The Ways of the Spirit*. New York: Crossroad, 1993.

Vanier, Jean. *Jesus, the Gift of Love*. New York: Crossroad, 1994.

Vennard, Jane E. *A Praying Congregation*. Herndon, Virginia: Alban Institute, 2005.

Wesley, John. Various works.

Wicks, Robert J. *Everyday Simplicity*. Notre Dame, Indiana: Sorin Books, 2000.

————. *Touching the Holy: Ordinariness, Self-Esteem, and Friendship*. Notre Dame, Indiana: Ave Maria Press, 2007.

Willard, Dallas. *The Divine Conspiracy: Rediscovering Our Hidden Life in God*. New York: HarperCollins, 1998.

————. *The Spirit of the Disciplines*. New York: HarperOne, 1990.

Williams, Clifford. *Singleness of Heart*. Grand Rapids, Michigan: Wm. B. Eerdmans, 1994.

Wolpert, Daniel. *Creating a Life With God*. Nashville: Upper Room Books, 2003.

————. *Leading a Life With God*. Nashville: Upper Room Books, 2006.

The Women of Magdalene with Becca Stevens. *Find Your Way Home*. Nashville: Abingdon Press, 2008. Used by permission.

LECTIONARY CHART

The weeks of the year are numbered from 1 to 56 (more readings than the number of weeks in the year allows for the variance in the date of Easter Sunday). The first reading begins with the first week of the Advent season. The chosen Scriptures follow the common lectionary and the church year, though the weekly readings can be read in any order. If you are following the church year, dates listed at the beginning of each weekly reading will help you move through the weeks. When no

	Year C 2009-2010	Year A 2010-2011	Year B 2011-2012
Week 1	Nov. 29, 2009	Nov. 28, 2010	Nov. 27, 2011
Week 2	Dec. 6, 2009	Dec. 5, 2010	Dec. 4, 2011
Week 3	Dec. 13, 2009	Dec. 12, 2010	Dec. 11, 2011
Week 4	Dec. 20, 2009	Dec. 19, 2010	Dec. 18, 2011
Week 5	Dec. 27, 2009	Dec. 26, 2010	Dec. 25, 2011
Week 6	Jan. 3, 2010	Jan. 2, 2011	Jan. 1, 2012
Week 7	Jan. 10, 2010	Jan. 9, 2011	Jan. 8, 2012
Week 8	Jan. 17, 2010	Jan. 16, 2011	Jan. 15, 2012
Week 9	Jan. 24, 2010	Jan. 23, 2011	Jan. 22, 2012
Week 10	Jan. 31, 2010	Jan. 30, 2011	Jan. 29, 2012
Week 11	Feb. 7, 2010	Feb. 6, 2011	Feb. 5, 2012
Week 12	——	Feb. 13, 2011	Feb. 12, 2012
Week 13	——	Feb. 20, 2011	——
Week 14	——	Feb. 27, 2011	——
Week 15	Feb. 14, 2010	March 6, 2011	Feb. 19, 2012
Week 16	Feb. 21, 2010	March 13, 2011	Feb. 26, 2012
Week 17	Feb. 28, 2010	March 20, 2011	March 4, 2012
Week 18	March 7, 2010	March 27, 2011	March 11, 2012
Week 19	March 14, 2010	April 3, 2011	March 18, 2012
Week 20	March 21, 2010	April 10, 2011	March 25, 2012
Week 21	March 28, 2010	April 17, 2011	April 1, 2012
Week 22	April 4, 2010	April 24, 2011	April 8, 2012
Week 23	April 11, 2010	May 1, 2011	April 15, 2012

date appears for a particular week, this signifies when you need to skip ahead until you find the desired date. If you are a member of a congregation following the Ecumenical Sunday Lectionary Scripture readings, you will likely hear the same Scripture read in worship on Sunday as the one you read in this daily guide. The chart below gives the week number and the liturgical date for each year listed.

Year C 2012-2013	Year A 2013-2014	Year B 2014-2015	Year C 2015-2016
Dec. 2, 2012	Dec. 1, 2013	Nov. 30, 2014	Nov. 29, 2015
Dec. 9, 2012	Dec. 8, 2013	Dec. 7, 2014	Dec. 6, 2015
Dec. 16, 2012	Dec. 15, 2013	Dec. 14, 2014	Dec. 13, 2015
Dec. 23, 2012	Dec. 22, 2013	Dec. 21, 2014	Dec. 20, 2015
Dec. 30, 2012	Dec. 29, 2013	Dec. 28, 2014	Dec. 27, 2015
Jan. 6, 2013	Jan. 5, 2014	Jan. 4, 2015	Jan. 3, 2016
Jan. 13, 2013	Jan. 12, 2014	Jan. 11, 2015	Jan. 10, 2016
Jan. 20, 2013	Jan. 19, 2014	Jan. 18, 2015	Jan. 17, 2016
Jan. 27, 2013	Jan. 26, 2014	Jan. 25, 2015	Jan. 24, 2016
Feb. 3, 2013	Feb. 2, 2014	Feb. 1, 2015	Jan. 31, 2016
——	Feb. 9, 2014	Feb. 8, 2015	——
——	Feb. 16, 2014	——	——
——	Feb. 23, 2014	——	——
——	——	——	——
Feb. 10, 2013	March 2, 2014	Feb. 15, 2015	Feb. 7, 2016
Feb. 17, 2013	March 9, 2014	Feb. 22, 2015	Feb. 14, 2016
Feb. 24, 2013	March 16, 2014	March 1, 2015	Feb. 21, 2016
March 3, 2013	March 23, 2014	March 8, 2015	Feb. 28, 2016
March 10, 2013	March 30, 2014	March 15, 2015	March 6, 2016
March 17, 2013	April 6, 2014	March 22, 2015	March 13, 2016
March 24, 2013	April 13, 2014	March 29, 2015	March 20, 2016
March 31, 2013	April 20, 2014	April 5, 2015	March 27, 2016
April 7, 2013	April 27, 2014	April 12, 2015	April 3, 2016

	Year C 2009-2010	**Year A** 2010-2011	**Year B** 2011-2012
Week 24	April 18, 2010	May 8, 2011	April 22, 2012
Week 25	April 25, 2010	May 15, 2011	April 29, 2012
Week 26	May 2, 2010	May 22, 2011	May 6, 2012
Week 27	May 9, 2010	May 29, 2011	May 13, 2012
Week 28	May 16, 2010	June 5, 2011	May 20, 2012
Week 29	May 23, 2010	June 12, 2011	May 27, 2012
Week 30	May 30, 2010	June 19, 2011	June 3, 2012
Week 31	——	——	——
Week 32	June 6, 2010	——	June 10, 2012
Week 33	June 13, 2010	——	June 17, 2012
Week 34	June 20, 2010	——	June 24, 2012
Week 35	June 27, 2010	June 26, 2011	July 1, 2012
Week 36	July 4, 2010	July 3, 2011	July 8, 2012
Week 37	July 11, 2010	July 10, 2011	July 15, 2012
Week 38	July 18, 2010	July 17, 2011	July 22, 2012
Week 39	July 25, 2010	July 24, 2011	July 29, 2012
Week 40	Aug. 1, 2010	July 31, 2011	Aug. 5, 2012
Week 41	Aug. 8, 2010	Aug. 7, 2011	Aug. 12, 2012
Week 42	Aug. 15, 2010	Aug. 14, 2011	Aug. 19, 2012
Week 43	Aug. 22, 2010	Aug. 21, 2011	Aug. 26, 2012
Week 44	Aug. 29, 2010	Aug. 28, 2011	Sept. 2, 2012
Week 45	Sept. 5, 2010	Sept. 4, 2011	Sept. 9, 2012
Week 46	Sept. 12, 2010	Sept. 11, 2011	Sept. 16, 2012
Week 47	Sept. 19, 2010	Sept. 18, 2011	Sept. 23, 2012
Week 48	Sept. 26, 2010	Sept. 25, 2011	Sept. 30, 2012
Week 49	Oct. 3, 2010	Oct. 2, 2011	Oct. 7, 2012
Week 50	Oct. 10, 2010	Oct. 9, 2011	Oct. 14, 2012
Week 51	Oct. 17, 2010	Oct. 16, 2011	Oct. 21, 2012
Week 52	Oct. 24, 2010	Oct. 23, 2011	Oct. 28, 2012
Week 53	Oct. 31, 2010	Oct. 30, 2011	Nov. 4, 2012
Week 54	Nov. 7, 2010	Nov. 6, 2011	Nov. 11, 2012
Week 55	Nov. 14, 2010	Nov. 13, 2011	Nov. 18, 2012
Week 56	Nov. 21, 2010	Nov. 20, 2011	Nov. 25, 2012

Year C 2012-2013	Year A 2013-2014	Year B 2014-2015	Year C 2015-2016
April 14, 2013	May 4, 2014	April 19, 2015	April 10, 2016
April 21, 2013	May 11, 2014	April 26, 2015	April 17, 2016
April 28, 2013	May 18, 2014	May 3, 2015	April 24, 2016
May 5, 2013	May 25, 2014	May 10, 2015	May 1, 2016
May 12, 2013	June 1, 2014	May 17, 2015	May 8, 2016
May 19, 2013	June 8, 2014	May 24, 2015	May 15, 2016
May 26, 2013	June 15, 2014	May 31, 2015	May 22, 2016
June 2, 2013	———	———	May 29, 2016
June 9, 2013	———	June 7, 2015	June 5, 2016
June 16, 2013	———	June 14, 2015	June 12, 2016
June 23, 2013	June 22, 2014	June 21, 2015	June 19, 2016
June 30, 2013	June 29, 2014	June 28, 2015	June 26, 2016
July 7, 2013	July 6, 2014	July 5, 2015	July 3, 2016
July 14, 2013	July 13, 2014	July 12, 2015	July 10, 2016
July 21, 2013	July 20, 2014	July 19, 2015	July 17, 2016
July 28, 2013	July 27, 2014	July 26, 2015	July 24, 2016
Aug. 4, 2013	Aug. 3, 2014	Aug. 2, 2015	July 31, 2016
Aug. 11, 2013	Aug. 10, 2014	Aug. 9, 2015	Aug. 7, 2016
Aug. 18, 2013	Aug. 17, 2014	Aug. 16, 2015	Aug. 14, 2016
Aug. 25, 2013	Aug. 24, 2014	Aug. 23, 2015	Aug. 21, 2016
Sept. 1, 2013	Aug. 31, 2014	Aug. 30, 2015	Aug. 28, 2016
Sept. 8, 2013	Sept. 7, 2014	Sept. 6, 2015	Sept. 4, 2016
Sept. 15, 2013	Sept. 14, 2014	Sept. 13, 2015	Sept. 11, 2016
Sept. 22, 2013	Sept. 21, 2014	Sept. 20, 2015	Sept. 18, 2016
Sept. 29, 2013	Sept. 28, 2014	Sept. 27, 2015	Sept. 25, 2016
Oct. 6, 2013	Oct. 5, 2014	Oct. 4, 2015	Oct. 2, 2016
Oct. 13, 2013	Oct. 12, 2014	Oct. 11, 2015	Oct. 9, 2016
Oct. 20, 2013	Oct. 19, 2014	Oct. 18, 2015	Oct. 16, 2016
Oct. 27, 2013	Oct. 26, 2014	Oct. 25, 2015	Oct. 23, 2016
Nov. 3, 2013	Nov. 2, 2014	Nov. 1, 2015	Oct. 30, 2016
Nov. 10, 2013	Nov. 9, 2014	Nov. 8, 2015	Nov. 6, 2016
Nov. 17, 2013	Nov. 16, 2014	Nov. 15, 2015	Nov. 13, 2016
Nov. 24, 2013	Nov. 23, 2014	Nov. 22, 2015	Nov. 20, 2016